Suffering: The Heart of the Matter

Life, God, suffering, and why my wife had a cardiac arrest

Paul Buller

Copyright © 2016 Paul Buller

All rights reserved.

ISBN: 1519676077
ISBN-13: 978-1519676078

DEDICATION

This book is dedicated, first and foremost, to Jesus; through his power and according to his will I am still able to make the second dedication.

I would also like to dedicate this book to my wife, Denise. Her cardiac arrest subjected me to several weeks of gut-wrenching heartache, but she's had to put up with being married to me for almost twenty years so I hope we're even.

To the staff at Denise's school for acting promptly and appropriately despite being scared out of their minds. To the paramedics, firemen and ER staff for not giving up, even after 73 minutes of resuscitation efforts.

To our parents, family, friends and church for their support during this terribly trying time in our lives. I could not possibly have survived this period in our family's history without their heroic intervention.

CONTENTS

Acknowledgements 1
Introduction 1
Section 1 5
A Grounded Hope 7
Why Bother with Prayer? 13
Some Perspective on the Problem of Suffering 17
Evil and Suffering in a Morally Good World 23
Imposed Virtues? 33
Objections: An Overview 39
Objection 1 – Too Much Suffering 43
Objection 2 – Suffering Is Unfairly Distributed 53
Objection 3 – Why Me? 59
Objection 4 – The Garden of Eden and Heaven 67
Objection 5 – Heroism Isn't Worth It 75
Objection 6 – Animal Suffering 83
Afterthoughts 93
Section 2 99
Perfect World – Introduction 101
Perfect World – The Offer 103
Perfect World – No Pain 109
Perfect World – No Harm 115
Perfect world – All Pleasure 123
Section 3 129
The Annals of Facebook 131

Acknowledgements

Evan Hertzsprung, my best friend, for his insights and feedback as I wrestled through these issues.

Elaine Phillips, my cheerful editor, who diligently persevered through the editorial process despite some suffering of her own at the time.

Tawa Anderson who, despite his unnaturally busy schedule, reviewed a significant portion of this book and brought his philosophical insights and life experience to bear on the subject. And for his extremely generous encouragement with respect to this project as a whole.

Introduction

This book is not intended to bring you comfort when you suffer.

Instead, this book is my attempt to understand suffering. I am an analytical kind of guy so this book is philosophical in nature. It explores abstract ideas. There is even a little ancient Greek in here. If you are enduring hardship right now, there are plenty of other books and resources intended to console during such times. My purpose for this book is quite different: I have questions. Is there meaning in suffering? Why would God allow so much of it? Why any at all? Is there a good purpose for suffering? Would the world be better or worse off if we could, hypothetically, eliminate suffering? I process life through writing, so when our family went through a difficult time it was inevitable that I would put pen to paper and approach the subject with these questions in mind.

Background

In 2013 my wife, Denise, suffered a cardiac arrest. For those without a medical background (like me) a cardiac arrest is unlike a heart attack in that the blood instantly stops flowing. The likelihood of full recovery rapidly diminishes to virtually nil unless intervention takes place within seconds or minutes. By some definitions a cardiac arrest is considered "death."

Late in the morning on April 16, 2013, my wife technically died between classes at the elementary school where she taught. She was alone when it happened and was found unconscious by her fellow teachers, slumped over her desk. Lifeless. Staff at her school called 9-1-1, and began CPR until the paramedics took over.

The short version of the rest of the story is as follows:

- From the time that we estimate she had the cardiac arrest until her heart was running reliably again was about 73 minutes.
- After her heart started running reliably again she was put into a medically induced coma and given "hypothermia treatment," meaning her body temperature was forcibly lowered. This was intended to help her brain recover from oxygen deprivation associated with being unconscious for so long during the event.
- This lasted for a couple of days after which the coma-inducing meds were slowly taken off.
- Then we waited to see if she would wake up. She did.
- We had to wait a few more days for her to recover enough to have her breathing tube removed so she could speak.
- Once she could speak again the question became, "How extensive is the neurological damage?" After a few days it became clear that the damage was minor and recoverable.
- She spent a total of about five weeks in the hospital working through rehabilitation before walking out under her own power.

Needless to say this period in our lives was very formative for our family. This is especially true of the first few days when she was in the medically induced coma. Would her heart quit again? Would they be able to restart it a second time? Not all people in a medically induced coma wake up; would she? The possibility of us planning a funeral was very real. If she did wake up, would she spend the rest of her life unable to function on her own?

During this time the subject of suffering was obviously front and centre in my mind. Having read about Christian apologetics before – this has been a longstanding passion of mine – I already had a conceptual framework through which to understand suffering and I had some vague theoretical concept of why God allows it, in principle. But living through some of what was (from my perspective) relatively intense suffering, I gained firsthand experience of that which I already knew, conceptually. That real-life experience brought my intellectual study into much sharper focus, and interestingly, my previous study of the subject provided a very unexpected sense of comfort through that situation.

Overview

This book is divided into three sections.

1) Drawing on this experience and my previous study of the subject, I wrote a series of articles for a website I blog at: blog.whyjesus.ca. The majority of this book is a compilation of those blog posts, slightly modified for book form (and polished as needed).

2) I have also included a short story I wrote entitled "Perfect World." This story puts the philosophical reflections into narrative form through a thought experiment. What if you could change the world and eliminate suffering? How would that work out?

3) Lastly, I included all the Facebook updates I posted during the time that Denise was in hospital, so you can read a fuller picture of the chain of events from her arrival, right to the day of her departure.

This book, therefore, attempts to consider the problem of suffering from three perspectives. For the analytical folks like me there are philosophical reflections. The same basic themes found in the reflections are also explored through a fictional thought experiment. And lastly suffering is viewed through the lens of a real-life example. You are invited to walk with us through the experience.

By way of quick clarification, the subjects of suffering and evil are intertwined (evil frequently produces suffering) but they are sufficiently different that they need to be considered separately. Evil necessarily involves a moral dimension whereas suffering is often amoral, as in when a tsunami strikes. Nobody is "to blame" for that, other than, perhaps, God himself. In this book I dedicate most of my attention to suffering and only touch on the subject of evil somewhat tangentially.

Section 1

Analytical reflections

A Grounded Hope

The kids and I had just burst through the door at around 11:25 on Tuesday April 16, 2013, when the phone rang. It was the principal at the school where my wife, Denise, taught. Considering who was calling and the trembling in her voice I knew there was only one reason we were talking.

My wife has lived with a heart condition for as long as I've known her (almost twenty years). She takes her medications religiously and her cardiac specialist has been keeping a watchful eye on her condition, but nobody was under any delusion that "all is well." We all knew of the very real potential that one day, for no apparent reason, Denise's heart might just get its wires crossed and she would collapse with virtually no warning at all. One day she would come face to face with her own mortality, possibly leaving behind a husband and two young children.

Today was that day.

When I arrived at the emergency room at the hospital I was immediately greeted by a social worker (not a good sign) and asked to wait in the family room instead of seeing Denise (another bad sign). My mother-in-law works at the hospital and she joined me shortly. We eventually did get to see Denise – an image of brokenness I will not describe and which I hope to one day forget. Yet, she was alive in a very generous sense of the word. A cardiac arrest is no small matter and the amount of work they had to put in to her body in order to resuscitate her meant a long and uncertain road to recovery. If she would recover at all. But when the ER was finished with her she had a pulse and was breathing. That was a start.

And so it began. We camped out in the family room of the Cardiac Intensive Care Unit at the hospital and the longest couch became my bed. The road to recovery was underway, but so many questions plagued all of us. Would she recover? To what extent? Because of the lack of oxygen to her brain for some unknown duration of time there was the very real possibility of neurological damage. How bad would it be? Could she recover from the damage? These were the questions few of us dared to ask and the doctors refused to answer.

As the hours and days passed and details of what happened were slowly sorted out, we began to get a picture of where we were and what the future might hold. My mother-in-law had a conversation with Denise's cardiologist after which she told me that the cardiologist was optimistic. Because Denise was probably only unconscious for a few minutes and because she received a very specific kind of treatment (I'll skip the details; they are technical and not immediately relevant), and given Denise's age and general health the cardiologist felt optimistic about her recovery.

"Besides," Denise's mom told me, "the doctor is just an optimistic kind of person."

I thought that was an interesting observation and it made me think about the optimism or pessimism I might harbour in my own mind. What kind of response am I experiencing? When I fear, why do I fear? When I feel hopeful, why am I hopeful?

When we first arrived at the hospital I had convinced myself of the very real possibility that we would end up planning a funeral. Why was that a concern for me? What reason did I have to be scared? Whenever we had talked with Denise's cardiologist she always made it clear that Denise's condition was not some minor blip on an otherwise spotless record of health. If her heart failed it would be instant, catastrophic and, if not treated almost immediately, fatal. I was very afraid, and not because I'm a fearful kind of guy. I had reason to fear. The facts were not in Denise's favour and my fear was a rational fear.

As Denise has been recovering I have become hopeful. I see improvements every day and the doctors and nurses continuously marvel at how fast and effective her recovery has been. She is regaining body functions on an almost hourly basis and is not showing any signs of long-term neurological damage. My hope, my optimism, is not due to my being an optimistic kind of guy. I don't hope just because I think that I ought to, or feel inclined to, or because it makes me feel better; I hope for the future because of what I see in the present and what I remember about the past.

I have nothing against Denise's cardiologist being an optimistic kind of person, but the only aspect of her optimism that I really care about is the optimism that is results-based. If she "feels" optimistic, good for her, but what does that offer, really, for Denise? Optimism based on feelings gets me nowhere; optimism based on the reality of the situation means something. Would she feel optimistic if a patient arrived in the emergency room with gunshot wounds to his head and chest, most of the blood drained from his body, and he had been without a pulse for the last two hours? Optimism would dry up pretty quickly in a situation like that because feelings only get you so far. If the reality of the situation conflicts with somebody's inherently optimistic nature, guess which one trumps the other?

But my optimism was rooted in more than the fact that Denise was unconscious for less than ten minutes (we don't know exactly how long). My optimism was rooted in more than the fact that she received high quality CPR and was rushed to the hospital. My optimism is rooted in more than the fact that the hospital has a reputation as one of the leading cardiac centres in North America, if not the world. My optimism is rooted in more than the fact that she received precisely the kind of treatment all the cardiologists hoped she would be able to receive, the absolutely best available today.

My optimism is also rooted in Jesus.

The moment news spread about Denise's situation, prayer chains were initiated, people were emailed, Facebook got a lot busier and hundreds of people started praying. In fact, we heard stories about people in the oddest circumstances with absolutely no known connection to either Denise or myself who gathered together and prayed for her recovery. Prayer was non-stop at times; 24-hour prayer vigils were set up.

What do we mean by "prayer?" If by prayer you are describing nothing more than the verbalization of your own thoughts and wishes then you need to pick a different word. What prayer really means is the act of taking your thoughts and wishes to somebody else. It is not a monologue but a dialogue. It involves you and somebody else, somebody other than mere mortals. When hundreds of people were praying about Denise they were not merely stating, out loud, that they hope she recovers. I hope so too and I could scream it from the roof of the hospital, but if nobody is listening then what's the point? Frankly our own hopes and dreams for the situation are, on their own, meaningless unless somebody with the ability to make a difference is listening.

But the prayers that many Christians were offering on Denise's behalf were not generic "prayers." Many people believe in the power of prayer; I do not. I believe only in the power of the one to whom we pray. If nobody is listening on the other end of the line, or if we "dialled the wrong number," what good is our prayer? Those who prayed were, by and large, devout Christians from many denominational backgrounds. In other words, it was not their prayers that were effective, but the fact that they were praying specifically to Jesus. No busy signal, no wrong number, and somebody picked up on the other end.

But why Jesus? Why am I so concerned that our prayers are offered to him and not to some other deity? Consider what I was asking for. I (and hundreds around me) wanted physical healing for Denise. Given her situation we knew that a positive outcome was unlikely; even one of the nurses called her "a miracle". We were all hoping for specific results at a specific time for a specific person. And those results, if it's not too much trouble, should be of a physical nature. I'm not asking for Denise to be at peace or have warm feelings; I want her body fixed. Plain and simple. The reason we were praying to Jesus is precisely because he has a record of delivering specific results at a specific time for specific people; results of a physical nature.

Some religions describe God as distant, uninvolved and more abstract than personal. Others describe him as somebody whose nature and decisions are absolutely beyond our comprehension and will seem whimsical and arbitrary to our feeble minds. But that is not how God has made himself known to humanity. When he incarnated among us in the person of Jesus, he made it clear that he was personal. He cared about us enough to denigrate himself to our level. He healed those around us and interacted with us in a way that was comprehensible to us. He made it clear that there is broad overlap between his priorities and ours. It is not a total overlap, of course, but his ways are not so foreign to us that we cannot possibly understand them.

Most importantly, though, he demonstrated his ability to get results. Physical results. Results within human history. Results that are often (but not always) consistent with what humans can comprehend and desire. When I pray, I am not merely going to verbalize my wishes to nobody in particular. I do not pray to a "god" that exists so far beyond humanity as to be unapproachable. I will not pray to a philosophical concept or a psychological crutch. No, I pray to the God who became human, was executed and buried in a cave and then picked himself up and walked out of that cave. That is the kind of God who has proven that he gets results. Physical results. Personal results. That fact of history – the resurrection of Jesus from the dead – is the grounding of my hope.

But the work of God is not limited to medical miracles. One of the staff asked if our family was Christian because we were handling this situation better than many. Although we were stressed and scared we still handled the situation with a greater calm than others do: another God-result. Indeed, studies have shown that folks with a religious frame of reference tend to have generally better psychological and physical health, including longevity, than those without. And those results even take into account factors like alcohol, smoking and so on.[1]

However, God is neither Santa Claus nor a vending machine. He does say no, sometimes, regardless of how fervently we ask. But as the research suggests he prefers to say yes whenever possible and, like us, he wants long life and health for the humanity he created. Of course he wants more than just that, but certainly no less. And when he says "no" then he will walk with us through that valley, too, giving us a strength that we would not have on our own. Another example of results that God provides, even if it is not the result we hoped for.

If you want real results then there is no God worth praying to other than the God who has a track record of getting results; the kind of God who willingly let his own creation execute him, and then confidently walked out of his own burial cave unassisted. When hundreds of Christians their faith specifically rooted in the risen Jesus, gathered together to pray for Denise, I had a results-based hope, not a wishful-thinking sort of hope, nor an I-am-just-a-hopeful-kind-of-guy sort of hope. God is willing and able to get results and he demonstrated this through Jesus. My hope was firmly grounded.

Is yours?

---

[1] Look up Dr. Harold Koenig for details; he has researched this subject extensively.

Why Bother with Prayer?

My wife's recovery from her cardiac arrest has been amazing and has inspired significant personal reflection. Hundreds of us (even some complete strangers) prayed for her full recovery. All indications are that she will fully recover despite the odds against her on several fronts. Indeed several of the staff have openly called her situation a miracle, an answer to prayer.[2]

But not everybody gets what they pray for. When we spent a few days in the Cardiac Intensive Care Unit at the hospital we saw, first-hand, the sobering reality that not all stories have happy endings. We saw two families say goodbye to loved ones, and two more families that appeared to be on the brink of farewells. While we rejoiced, many others on that unit mourned and openly wept. I'm sure many of those families prayed like we did. God said yes to Denise. God said no to them.

Some time ago I was called on to speak at a church where the pastor and his family had recently buried their child. She was born with serious health issues and they were told that she would only live a few weeks or months, but she lasted a year and a half. Despite what the doctors told them, prayers were offered for some kind of miracle that would give her a long life and health.

But God said no.

---

[2] I usually resist the urge to refer to this as a miracle because I'm a bit of a stickler for using words properly. Though God was clearly active I'm not so sure this technically constitutes a miracle in the philosophically accurate sense of the word. I'm using the word somewhat more loosely in this chapter.

Let this hit a little closer to home for a minute. Denise's dad died of heart complications when she was roughly two years old. As an interesting subplot to this entire drama of our lives, the Cardiac Intensive Care Unit where Denise was being treated was the exact same unit her dad was initially admitted for treatment. Countless prayers were offered up for his return to health over the course of time that his life slowly slipped away. In fact, when he died he was roughly the same age that Denise, his daughter, was when she visited that same unit. He left behind a wife with two kids and another on the way. Denise would have left behind a husband and two kids. Many people begged God for his life as they begged for Denise's life.

But God said no.

Indeed countless other examples of human tragedy could easily be offered up. Perhaps you even have such a story. An abusive or unfaithful spouse that you pray will change their ways. Employment that is desperately needed yet never to be found. Health problems. Relational breakdowns. Let's get really morbid and consider countless incidents of murder, genocide, torture, modern-day sexual slavery, aborted babies, serial killers, terrorists and so much more. We pray for a different world. We beg. We plead. We get on our knees and weep in the hope that God will fix everything. Or if not everything, at least our specific situation.

But God says no. What are we to make of that?

The mystery of why God allows the world to remain in its imperfect state, and why he sometimes answers our prayers in ways we desperately wish he would not have answered them, are serious questions worth wrestling with. We will consider those questions later in this book. Right now I want to consider why we pray when we know that God will not always answer our prayers in the way we would prefer. I want to consider that question by way of analogy.

When Denise was found unconscious by her co-workers they immediately called 9-1-1 and were instructed to begin CPR. Suppose they knew the statistics associated with cardiac arrests. When a person has a cardiac arrest outside of a hospital the odds of their recovery, even if given all the best treatment, is roughly five to seven percent.[3] Only about one in twenty people will survive a cardiac arrest if you give them CPR until the paramedics arrive with a defibrillator (as in Denise's case). Nineteen times out of twenty they will die anyway, no matter how much effort you put in, how sincere you are in your efforts or how perfect your technique is.

---

[3] The odds are significantly better if an AED is nearby. There was no AED in Denise's school.

Those are pretty lousy odds. Given those odds of success, would a reasonable person who sees somebody with a cardiac arrest just shrug their shoulders and walk by the victim with the mindset, "Oh, well, CPR almost certainly wouldn't have helped them"? Even in the face of discouragingly low odds of success, people begin CPR anyway – at least those with half an ounce of humanity in them do. We do so because we know that, even if CPR fails, there is at least a chance of success, but if CPR is not administered then death is one hundred percent certain. The only hope for recovery in the face of a cardiac arrest is CPR and a defibrillator, even if that hope is a faint and distant hope. So we begin CPR because we are focused on the hope, not on the likelihood of success.

Should we not approach God in a similar manner? We ask God for a miracle because we know he is the only one capable of providing the miracle we ask for, whether he chooses to provide it or not. Even though we are aware that he might say "no" to our plea, and even if the odds of him saying "yes" are astonishingly low, we ought to ask anyway. We ought to ask with all the sincerity, dedication and effort that Denise's co-workers put into the CPR they gave her. They did not do CPR because they knew it would work; they did CPR because they knew it was the only action that could possibly work. They didn't know it would work; they hoped it might work. Similarly we pray with the greatest sincerity and dedication, and we boldly ask for the greatest and most shocking possible outcome, not because we know ahead of time that God will provide a miracle, but because if there is going to be a miracle it will come from him. We hope in him whether he answers or not.

CPR is just a physical act performed on a physical body. It has no will or consciousness. It neither knows the victim nor cares about them. God, on the other hand, is personal. He has a will. He understands and loves the person lying unconscious on the ground. As the Bible reminds us, God is a loving father who delights in giving us what we ask for (Matthew 7:7–11). Though he will not always give us what we pray for – sometimes he has a bigger picture in mind that precludes this particular miracle or that one – it is his preference to give us a long and fulfilled life with which to honour and serve him. It is his preference to surprise us with the miraculous. If we have hope enough to attempt the impersonal and merely physical act of CPR, given the incredibly low odds of success, why would we not ask our conscious, personal and loving God to intervene in our situations with the most glorious and astonishing of miracles? How much more powerful is he than mere CPR?

One Bible story that has been very relevant to me during this entire episode has been the story of David losing his son.[4] In this story David is told that God is going to kill his son and also the reason why: David's sin. Despite knowing God's plan, and despite knowing the reason behind God's plan, David prays with far more dedication and sincerity than I would dare guess any of us have ever prayed in our lives. When we pray, we do not know what God's plans are. When David prayed he did know God's plans and he begged God to change his plans. In David's case God went ahead with his plans and gave David "no" for an answer. But what has always struck me about that story is David's dedication to asking God anyway, knowing full well that his request is almost one hundred percent guaranteed to be declined. He didn't just ask, he starved himself for a week and lay in the dirt as a sign of his recognition of his sinful nature and of his place before God.

How many of us would pray like that when we do not know God's plan, never mind when we are praying that God would change his plans? David puts me to shame!

Furthermore, when God did finalize his "no," David did not curse him or walk away from the faith; he went up to the Temple and worshipped. I doubt he was singing happy songs about how God always made him glad (we have too many songs like that these days!) but he approached God with an attitude of profound worship nonetheless. Do we have so much integrity that our faith will stand firm even if God does not give us everything we want and ask for? Will we continue to worship God when he refuses to play Santa Claus? Or will we take the approach of Job's wife: "Curse God and die!"[5]

I am humbled and delighted that hundreds of people (I am not exaggerating) asked God for a miracle for Denise. Though I am painfully aware that he does often say "no," he decided to say "yes" this time. Even if many families live with disappointment and loss when God answers no (my wife's family being one of them when Denise's dad died many years ago), surely we can celebrate when he does say yes and surely we ought to ask for a miracle even when he will almost certainly say no" David prayed for a "yes" when he was told ahead of time that God would say "no." We should be so bold! We ask, not because we are confident that he will give us what we want, but because if there is going to be a miracle, he is the only means by which it could happen.

When we pray, go big or go home!

---

[4] 2 Samuel 12:1–23.

[5] Job 2:9.

Some Perspective on the Problem of Suffering

This world is pretty messed up, isn't it? Corrupt governments. War zones around the world. Murder, rape and genocide fill the nightly news. That doesn't even cover natural disasters like floods, fires and hurricanes. Yep, the world is a pretty messed up place.

Of course, it is also a very beautiful place. People get married every day. Children play in the park. The sun shines, rain nourishes the earth, and trees are filled with delightful fruit for our enjoyment. Yeah, the world is a pretty great place. And it is messed up.

In this chapter I want to consider how our perspective on pain and suffering influences the conclusions we draw from it. Having your heart stop without any warning, having your chest pounded on for roughly an hour in an attempt to restart it, having shocks of electricity forced across your torso countless times, being medically paralyzed and sedated as your body temperature is forcibly lowered several degrees Celsius, and then having to recover from all the above constitutes, in my humble opinion, a reasonable dose of suffering. Hardly the worst this world has seen, but severe enough to get our attention.

When considering the prevalence of suffering in the world, many people wonder where God fits into all of that. It seems to me that is a perfectly legitimate question. Indeed I wonder, sometimes, why so many Christians seem to have a theology of "God wants me to be happy all the time" when the Bible is replete with examples of people suffering specifically as a result of their willingness to obey God. Does God tend to bless those who trust in him? Absolutely, but that is far from the whole story. Sometimes he puts his loved ones in harm's way for very specific reasons: either personal growth through trial or for the betterment of somebody else. Suffering is unquestionably a facet of the reality we find ourselves in, and we ought to take it seriously.

But not too seriously. Suffering should be treated with a seriousness that is proportional to its place in the world. We should not try to sweep it under the rug, nor should we try to stick it behind a magnifying glass and blow it out of proportion. Indeed, while some Christians may downplay the reality of suffering in our world, I dare say there are others who see nothing but horror and tragedy everywhere they look. The earth, we are told, is blood-soaked – a melodramatic representation of reality if there ever was one.

This tendency to misrepresent the scale of suffering was made all the more apparent to me as I watched my wife emerge from her medically induced coma and start to re-engage the world. As a result of her cardiac arrest she suffered some minor neurological damage and, in all likelihood, some parts of her brain were still experiencing some excess pressure which distorted her innate perspective on life. When she awoke from her coma there was an undeniably negative tone in her response to the situation she found herself in. Was such negativity understandable? Yes, but it was still out of character for her.

Let me give an example. Several days after she came to, she started walking. At one point the physiotherapists were doing various tests on the state of her recovery. They had her walk to the window in her room, look out, and tell them what she saw. I'll give you a sneak peek. From that particular window the edge of the hospital property was a stone's throw away. There was some kind of mechanical building slightly to the right and another hospital tower a little further on. In the centre and to the other side the terrain opened up to a wide valley that had been carved by the river that flows through our city. Trees covered the earth as far as we could see. In the distance the other side of the valley rose, but not so high as to block the Rocky Mountains that capped the horizon. It was a sunny day with few clouds; the kind of day that beckoned one outdoors for some walking and biking.

What did she see? "Hospital stuff," she said, with a slightly disgruntled tone.

Seriously? You've got the sun playing peek-a-boo with the clouds, trees blanketing the landscape, the Rocky Mountains framing this entire picture and all you can see is the hospital stuff in the foreground and to the side? This is an example of what we might call "selection bias." When a person is expecting to see something, they tend to find it wherever they look. While Denise's brain was recovering it went through a stage where she was unnaturally pessimistic and frustrated with everything. In that state even the most glamorous piece of heavenly artwork – namely our beautiful city and the surrounding countryside – is drowned by the horror and ugliness of a little bit of hospital architecture in the foreground.[6]

There is another aspect of this whole situation that led to Denise's negative perspective. When she collapsed from her cardiac arrest she was clinically dead. That is a terrifying thought when you let it sink in. Many factors weighed against her recovery – the odds were not in her favour – but she unexpectedly pulled through and appears to be on the road to more or less a full neurological recovery. Whether that is a miracle or not in the technical sense of the word is a subject for another day, but suffice it to say that all of us – family, therapists, nurses and doctors – are stunned with not only the fact of her virtually perfect recovery, but the speed at which she is racing toward it.

But not her. When she first woke up she had short-term memory issues. Sometimes I would have to tell her several times a day that she had a cardiac arrest, and I would have to remind her about the CPR, the ambulance ride, ER and so forth. She will never remember the actual events, of course, but she was having difficulty remembering that I had described the events to her. She kept forgetting why she was in the hospital in the first place.

When she looked at her situation – she could not walk, she could not feed herself, she could not write coherent English – she did not see events through the lens of "I was technically dead just last week." Instead, she saw through the lens of "I never used to have any of these problems." Her memory did not include the valley she had just passed through; because of her short-term memory problems she could only remember where she used to be before all of this happened. Her mind was constantly hitting "reset," so she kept comparing her immediate state to her normal state without taking into consideration what she had just been through. From that perspective she was experiencing a constant deficit of sorts, and that's all

---

[6] In the spring of 2016, Denise had some unexpected episodes with her heart that required a brief stay in the hospital. She once again found herself in the same cardiac unit she was in the first time around, in a room on the same side of the building as before. In short, she once again had the same view.

When she was in that room in 2013, her memory had not yet recovered, so in 2016 she had no long-term memory of being in that room. Nor does she remember our conversation about the view from that room. When I saw that she had the same view, and knowing she likely didn't remember, I casually commented on it. Denise replied that the view outside the window was amazing.

Same view, different perspective.

she would see at first. The rest of us constantly compared her current progress to the state she was in when she arrived in the ER. When seen through that lens we were in a constant state of joy and excitement at her progress. Bewildered at our enthusiasm, she only saw through her lens and lived in a virtually constant state of frustration and pessimism because of everything she could not do.

For two reasons – neurological damage to the brain interrupting her normal personality, and short-term memory issues giving her a unique frame of reference – she tended to see her situation in a far more negative light than any of us around her did. We were delighted; she was aggravated. She was experiencing selection bias with respect to her circumstances because she was unable to see the whole picture.

All too often those who shake their fists at God because of all the suffering in the world are exhibiting symptoms of selection bias similar to what Denise went through. I am well aware that some people have had a really rough go at life – they have suffered far more than the rest of us could possibly imagine – but even in those situations it is not necessary that one must see the world through the eyes of pessimism and frustration. For the most part we choose our lens unless, like Denise, we are dealing with neurological issues. Of course there are certainly some forms of suffering so extensive and so severe that it is virtually impossible for any person to maintain a positive disposition. But how many of us are in that boat?

What I have found interesting over the years of observing people is the inconsistency of responses that people have to their own suffering. There are those who develop a negative outlook on life as a result of their suffering, and this would seem to be the most understandable response. But there are so many exceptions. Others who suffer do not exhibit that tendency at all. Some swing in the opposite direction as they begin to marvel at the wonder of life as seen anew through fresh eyes. At the very end of the book *The Problem of Pain* by C. S. Lewis there is an appendix written by a medical doctor (R. Havard, MD) based on his observations of those who have endured various forms of pain. He ends his insightful little commentary with the note, "Pain provides an opportunity for heroism; the opportunity is seized with surprising frequency." Some who suffer interpret their suffering through the lens of negativity, but others who suffer rise to the occasion and set an example for the rest of us.

While I find the responses of those who suffer fascinating, what I find even more amazing is how many people get so remarkably hung up on the suffering in the world while they live in relative comfort. They have their health. They have their sanity. They have the financial means to meet their needs and many of their desires as well. They live in middle- to upper-class houses. They are nowhere near a war zone and there is no volcano or hurricane zone within a day's drive of where they live. They get to choose their government and will not be sent to jail without due process. They are free to express themselves without fear of police intervention.

Yet they see the world through the lens of negativity. They see the suffering of others and it becomes their frame of reference for all of life. Because other people suffer they shake their fists at God. Where is he? Why does he not fix the world? Why do so many bad things happen? All fair questions, absolutely, but the persistence with which they ask their questions often reveals more about the questioner than it does about God, the only one qualified to answer them. Like my wife who gazed upon a serene image of natural beauty in the distance but could only see the hospital property at the end of her nose, many people choose the lens of negativity as their frame of reference for the world around them and refuse to see all the splendour and majesty that engulfs us daily.

If we have grounds to shake our fist at God because of what is wrong with the world, should we not (to be consistent) embrace him with gratitude when we stumble upon all that is right with the world? If we have good reason to conclude God does not exist because there is pain, do we not have equally good reason to conclude that God does exist because there is pleasure? We are moved to tears and anguish when we hear about injustice and heartache, but are we equally moved to tears of joy and delight when the beauty of the world and the love of humanity overwhelms us? Or do we even allow the beauty of the world to touch us in any meaningful way? Perhaps the only emotions some experience are emotions of horror and anger. More selection bias.

To properly tackle the problem of pain and all of its philosophical implications, it seems to me, one must be prepared to dedicate equal time and attention to the problem of pleasure and follow that evidence where it leads. One must consider the whole picture, not just those parts of the picture that we see because of the lens we have chosen to look through. The world is broken – absolutely and unequivocally broken – but it is also very beautiful.

Evil and Suffering in a Morally Good World

The question of why God allows evil and suffering is, not surprisingly, a question as old as the hills upon which people have committed evil and have suffered. To presume that I can answer the question with any kind of final authority would be the highest form of a delusion of grandeur, but I hope to shed some light on the fact that a world in which moral good is even possible must be a world in which evil and suffering are also possible. In fact, challenges of some sort must exist for certain virtues to even possibly exist. Of course God's reasons for making this world in particular are probably infinitely more complex than we can imagine, but I hope I can unpack one of his countless reasons for certain features of our world. Even if I succeed, this will hardly be an exhaustive account of God's intentions for our world.

In the first few days after Denise arrived in the hospital we weren't actually sure she was going to make it at all. The experience was terrifying as we watched her on the brink of death, followed by weeks of recovery from brain damage. During our time in the hospital I got a glimpse of the various other medical challenges that people face. I saw part of the face of suffering, although by no means all of it. It was personal. Given all my years of experience in apologetics, and given the virtually constant barrage of "God is a horrible monster because people suffer" message that I'm used to hearing, I had that context floating around in the back of my mind the entire time. I was expecting to have to deal with a serious crisis of faith as I began facing, in a deeply personal way, the very feature of our universe that so many atheists claim makes belief in God inherently irrational. I have to admit, I wondered whether my relatively sheltered and comfortable life had insulated me from the harsh realities of the world, and whether faith could withstand the winds of real life.

The suffering that our family went through, and the suffering that I saw other people go through, made me realize something very important. For all my talk with other people about the subject of suffering, I hadn't really faced a lot of it.[7] It was easy to speak of suffering in abstract terms, but once I was actually in it – once it became a real part of my life – the entire picture changed. I saw suffering, yes, and it was horrifying. But I saw something else that is virtually never discussed when folks dialogue about evil and suffering. I saw something so beautiful, born as it was out of suffering, that I was stunned I'd never noticed it before. Something that not only happened to come out of suffering, but could only, even in theory, come into being through suffering. I saw a flower once I stopped staring at the dirt. A hypothetical world devoid of any hardship of any kind would mean losing a very magnificent baby as we threw it out with the bathwater.

So let's put our thinking caps on. Let's start by imagining a world without one of the most common causes of suffering: pain.[8]

No pain, no gain

Surely a pain-free world would be better than a world with pain, wouldn't it? Imagine if you stubbed your toe and you didn't feel any pain. I stub my toes a lot so I have to agree that, at first glance, a pain-free world sounds pretty good. What possible reason could there be to maintain the reality of pain in our world? What possible good could it serve?

To answer that question we can ask those with congenital insensitivity to pain, a condition that prevents some people from ever experiencing pain. Wouldn't that be nice?

While at first the inability to feel pain may sound like a gift, the opposite is true. When babies grow, they experiment with their surroundings. When they feel pain, they learn that something is bad for them and stop doing it.

Not those children who have congenital insensitivity to pain. Examples of what these babies and kids do to themselves include breaking bones without feeling what they did, poking their eyes with their fingers, and biting their own tongues.

Oh, my. That doesn't sound so good after all. As I explored this subject

---

[7] And to be perfectly clear, let me emphasize that the suffering our family went through is a far, far cry from the magnitude of suffering many other people in the world are forced to endure.

[8] In my quest to imagine a pain-free world I wrote a short story called "Perfect World." I have included it later in this book.

on the internet I also discovered some further drawbacks to a lack of pain sensitivity. If people with this condition survive to adulthood (most don't) and happen to contract some other disease, they probably will not know about it until it is too late. For instance, if a healthy person gets cancer they may know that something is wrong because they feel an unusual pain in a certain place on their body. If caught early enough – in other words if they experience the pain early enough – many forms of cancer can be treated. Somebody with no ability to feel pain would never know they had cancer until it had spread too far to be treated.

When we pop some pills to alleviate pain, what we do, practically speaking, is temporarily silence the alarm that is telling us something is wrong. Silencing the alarm is a good thing, but if we never had that alarm in the first place then we would never be aware something was wrong. Indeed, a great deal of medical diagnosis involves questions like, "Where does it hurt?" and "Can you describe the pain?" The types and magnitudes of pain all mean something; they are like instruments in our body. Lacking a pain alarm would be (and for some people, it is) catastrophic. Generally speaking, pain is something we should be grateful for, not something we should want to get rid of. When pain functions properly it both enhances and lengthens human life.

Imagine if, tomorrow morning, every human on the face of the earth stopped sensing pain. Children would rarely grow to adulthood. Adults would die off far more rapidly than we presently do. Civilization as we know it would cease to exist in one, maybe two generations. Should we dream of a pain-free world? Not if we have any moral sanity. Wave goodbye to the very prospect of octogenarians and, eventually, the very prospect of the human race in any form. No, a world lacking pain of any kind (assuming it is still possible to be harmed) is an objectively horrifying world relative to our present world.

Pain, it turns out, is an unexpected blessing. More unexpected results ahead…

I'm invincible!

But, it could be objected, what if we never felt pain and we never got diseases and could never be hurt and could never die? No starvation. No gunshot wounds. No suicides. No decapitations. In other words, what if we were invincible? In that case there would be no need for pain and we would also never be injured or die. That sounds like a pretty good alternative, right? Given what our family went through when my wife was on the brink of death I have to say this concept, on the face of it, sounds magnificent! .

Indeed, a world in which we could never be even slightly injured does sound appealing. As well as the advantage of a total lack of self-inflicted (and nature-inflicted) suffering, there is the added advantage of a total lack of evil-inflicted suffering. So many human tragedies come to mind. If humans could neither be injured nor killed we would have had no Holocaust. There would be no 9/11. No terrorist attacks. No murders, rapes, mothers drowning their children, boyfriends beating their girlfriends, abortions or any other of a host of evils that plague our day and age.

This all sounds like an unqualified blessing until we consider that we have been stripped of our moral freedom. You see, moral evil is but one side of the two-sided coin we call moral freedom. If I follow the logic of Henry Ford who once quipped that his customers could have a car in any colour they wanted so long as it was black, and I say that people can make their own moral choices so long as they always make the morally right choice, then I have, practically speaking, eliminated their choice. Without the ability to do moral wrong we would not have true moral freedom.

Thus, in a world devoid of pain, harm and death, moral evil is impossible. Without the possibility of making a morally evil choice – killing somebody, starving them, and so on – morality itself is rendered meaningless. The upside to that, of course, is that there would be absolutely no moral evil. But is there a downside?

[There is another element to all this I'm skipping over for the sake of brevity: the ability to emotionally and psychologically harm a person. I am only considering the physical aspect of this for now, but a similar line of reason would apply to non-physical forms of moral choices.]

Evil-free world – the fine print

Surely we can all agree that an inability to do moral evil would be fabulous, right? I mean, honestly, if we could only ever be kind to each other wouldn't that be a good thing? Indeed, in such a world everything we ever did would be good because bad could not exist, even in principle. Perhaps we should gladly hand over moral meaning if that would result in a complete avoidance of evil. The very concept sounds like a blissful utopia until we think a little further about all the implications.

Would it be morally evil to withhold food from a person? Of course! They could starve. Feeding them, though, is a moral good. Would that still be the case in a world where starvation was impossible? Not only was starvation impossible, no person could ever, even theoretically, experience the discomfort of hunger. We would neither feel the need to eat, nor would we suffer any consequences if we did not eat. You could either withhold food or you could shower them with food; either way your actions are irrelevant. Is it possible to be evil? No. Is it possible to be good? Also, no.

Or suppose you shoved a blind old woman in front of a moving vehicle. What a heinous act! Instead of shoving her in front of a moving vehicle you should help her cross the street so she does not accidentally get struck by a careless driver. But in a world without danger or death, would it matter either way? You could push as many people as you wanted in front of vehicles; there would be no consequence. And if you helped the blind person avoid a collision, that would serve absolutely no purpose; it's not as if they could ever be injured.

In a world where I am unable to physically hurt somebody (moral evil), nothing I do could physically benefit them either (moral good). In a world without danger or death we lose the ability to hurt somebody, but we also lose the ability to help them. Without moral meaning we lose not only moral evil, we also lose moral good. Vice is gone, but so is virtue.

Where have all the heroes gone?

Let's take a closer look at the concept of moral good. What are some characteristics that people intuitively recognize as virtues? Love, courage, kindness, patience, self-sacrifice, integrity, a passion for justice, personal discipline and many more. These are the kinds of things that define people of honour, of dignity. In many cases we call people who exhibit these traits "heroes." They often sacrifice their own comfort, resources and sometimes even their safety and their very lives for the sake of others facing personal hardship. In other cases, heroes face personal hardship themselves, enduring that hardship with honour, their heads held high and their dignity intact. They grab life by the horns and make the most of whatever hand they have been dealt. These are the people we look up to and respect. These people represent the pinnacle of what it means to be human. They are role models for the rest of us.

These heroes, I came to realize, are the people who saved my wife's life. The 9-1-1 operator who coached my wife's colleagues through CPR. My wife's colleagues who were scared out of their minds but dove in and administered CPR on their clinically dead colleague, their friend. The paramedics and firemen who responded to the call. The doctors and nurses in the ER who dedicated the better part of an hour doing everything they could for her heart. Other doctors and nurses who worked to restore her to full health.

I cannot imagine the picture my wife's colleagues stared at as they pounded on the chest of their technically dead friend. Fear must have gripped them, but they heroically muscled right through the fear and horror. The medical staff and paramedics have accepted careers with lousy hours (shift work), insufficient pay in some cases, high stress, and emotional trauma associated with watching people die on a regular basis, as well as a host of other difficulties and hardships. But they chose these careers. They signed up. They go to their jobs day in and day out, sometimes sacrificing their personal sanity for the benefit of others. Can any reasonable person look at these magnificent people and not agree that they represent the best of what it means to be human? These people, dozens of them, who saved my wife's life demonstrated such character, such nobility and personal beauty. These are the flowers that sprout from the dirt that was my wife's cardiac arrest.

The thing with heroism – being a person of virtue – is that we are not born with it; rather, we grow into it over the course of our lives. Indeed, it would be logically impossible to be "born a hero" (see the next chapter for more details). It simply takes time and experience. Let me illustrate. Enduring personal hardship is the only logically possible means by which one could develop the virtue of perseverance. One does not "persevere" in a setting of absolute bliss; the very idea is irrational. Courage is only possible in a world occupied with real dangers that one might fear. Personal discipline is impossible if everything we desired was immediately available without any effort at all. It is logically impossible for a person to become the kind of hero who places himself in harm's way in a world absolutely devoid of harm. These are simple definitional matters; no fancy philosophy here. Many virtues are logically impossible in the absence of any challenges or hardships.

A world without moral good – a world without danger or suffering, as described earlier – is also a world without heroes. It becomes a world without honour, without dignity; a world within which no human possesses any of the virtues that represent the pinnacle of human potential. In what some might consider to be the "perfect world," no human could possibly ever develop any character of any kind, good or bad. Everything that makes the human experience a rich, meaningful experience would be absolutely impossible in such a world.

We would have no epic tales of soldiers defending their homeland in the face of insurmountable foes. We would never be inspired by the bravery of our police as they face a lone gunman with deadly aim. We would have no folklore of brave knights and damsels in distress. Romeo and Juliet? Gone. War and Peace. Never heard of it. All the great dramas of the world – indeed much of what makes the human experience a rich tapestry – would be completely absent. I'm not well versed in the arts, literature and music, but a friend of mine more acquainted with these assured me that many of the finest examples of human expression would never have been expressed in a world devoid of evil and suffering. The richest examples of human imagination become conceptually impossible.

Even the everyday examples of self-sacrifice on a smaller scale – spouses who commit to relationships built on healthy compromise (i.e. it's not always about me anymore), and parents who feed, bath and clothe their children to keep them alive, healthy and warm – would all be rendered either pointless or would disappear altogether. After all, if a newborn infant could not possibly contract a disease due to unsanitary conditions, or starve, or freeze to death – indeed the child could not even experience discomfort – what's to stop a parent from abandoning a child? Indeed, what possible motive is there to care for the child in the first place? Every possible form of heroism, even down to the overlooked heroism of parenting as we understand it, would become logically impossible in such a world. As a world without lines cannot possible have triangles, so a world without challenges cannot possibly have heroes.

At an even more basic level, no human would have any need whatsoever to go to work. Whether or not I eat, either way I experience no pain, and I never die. Whether or not I have a house, either way I will never freeze to death in winter nor overheat in the sweltering summer. In fact, I would never even feel discomfort from hot or cold. Followed to its logical extreme, it would be unfathomable that human civilization as we know it would possibly have emerged. Even if some small handful of humans felt unusually inspired to study science, for instance, who would be bothered to build their scientific instruments? The entire infrastructure of science, medicine, art, economics, governments, literature, education, nations and so on would be completely absent. Humanity would be reduced to a featureless blob of homogeneous inactivity.

Those who would rid the world of pain, suffering and the possibility of evil – those who demand that God should have made the world a "better" place – are implicitly seeking a world without heroes. A virtue-free world. But is that really better? Maybe they never realized it before, but now that the costs have been laid on the table, surely we all instinctively understand the gaping absence that would characterize such a world. Moral good, after all, is not merely an abstract concept; it is a life-defining experience. Hopefully we all know people in our lives, usually the elderly, who are profoundly mature. They are the deep souls, the sages. They have a maturity about them not measured in years and a beauty in their being that defies their wrinkles. Talk to such people. Ask them about their lives. Many of them have faced hardship. Many of them have made a life of helping others. Ask them what the most formative events in their lives were and you will probably hear stories of difficulty and challenges. They have faced the ugliness of life and have turned that external ugliness into an inner beauty that outshines its source. Like a fire that burns brighter than the spark that ignites it, the tragedy of all that is wrong with the world is easily surpassed by the magnificence of those who have become the greatest souls our race has ever seen. You can be one of these honourable pinnacles of humanity, too, if you choose the right attitude toward the hardship you see in your own life and the lives of those around you. Will you rise to the occasion or descend into self-pity? Tragedy can make a person better or bitter, but a total absence of hardship of any kind, even an unwillingness to dedicate yourself to helping others through their hardship, condemns you to a state of existential irrelevance.

In a "perfect world" you could never grow into what these heroes have become. In a "perfect world" these heroes of our race could not possibly have become the honourable sages they are. Sit down with such people, treat them to coffee and learn about their lives. Really get to know them. If you say the world is better off without evil and suffering, you are also saying that the world is better off without them. I cannot bring myself to say that.

As I sat next to my wife – who was connected to countless tubes and wires, her life hanging in the balance – I experienced the same natural yearning for a "better" world that every morally sane human does. But I now understand that a world devoid of such trauma is not necessarily better, on the whole, than a world where our family must go through an experience like that.

In conclusion

Thus we find:

- A world where humans have the opportunity to become heroes is superior to a world where heroism is logically impossible.
- Heroism, and moral good in general, is only logically possible in a world where moral evil is logically possible.
- Moral evil is only possible in a world where harm and suffering are possible.
- In a world where harm and suffering are possible, pain generally improves and protects life.

Thus it seems to me that pain, suffering and evil must all necessarily be real possibilities in a world where moral virtue, and moving toward the fulfillment of the human potential for heroism, is logically possible. Though there may be some who believe God, in his divine omnipotence, can just get rid of pain as easily as we pop a couple of pills, such dreamworlds are inherently simplistic. God certainly could do that, but getting rid of pain – though it seems trivially simple – entails a wider array of unintended consequences that would reduce the entire human experience either to an unimaginable horror or utter irrelevance. Those who make such demands are inadvertently asking for a world devoid of any real significance or meaning. No civilization. No work. No virtues. No character. No dignity. No honour. Nothing but the most horrifying display of unadulterated hedonism we could possibly fathom. It comes down to a choice between heroism and hedonism. Selflessness or selfishness.

Consider with me the paradoxical wisdom of G. K. Chesterton: "Meaninglessness comes not from being weary of pain, but from being weary of pleasure."

[In researching this subject a fellow apologist pointed me to John Hick's book *Evil and the God of Love*. In it is found the concept of "soul making," an idea obviously similar to what I have described. While he and I arrive at similar conclusions, I think the phrase "soul making" makes the entire process sound like a manufacturing factory instead of the awe-inspiring and spiritually rewarding process it really is. Also, I should point out that I deeply disagree with Hick on various other issues (like universalism), so this may be one of the few places where our thoughts overlap.]

Imposed Virtues?

As I worked through these concepts on suffering and why God allows it, from several places I have found some resistance to the idea that suffering, hardship and challenges are necessary for character formation. The objection, briefly, is that God should have just "made us virtuous" from the start, skipped all that part about suffering and unpleasantness and just landed us in Heaven. I have tried to argue that virtues are the kinds of things that cannot be implanted fully formed, they must be grown through life experience. I have argued, in fact, that it would be logically impossible for God to implant virtues. This means our world – ugliness, brokenness and all – is logically necessary if any human is to become virtuous.

I was poking around a bit to see if I was off my rocker. It's always a good idea to see if experts in the field agree with you or not, especially if you are in my position; unequivocal non-expert. I looked up "Virtue Ethics" in *The Stanford Encyclopedia of Philosophy*.[9] I'll be upfront here: the article does not directly address this question of the hypothetical scenario of having virtues implanted and I am not claiming that it does. However, what it does say about virtue ethics is worth considering vis-à-vis this question.

First, there is a word that needs to be learned here – *eudaimonia*. It's Greek and I am no expert but I think it's pronounced You-Day-Moan-E-Uh. As described in the article:

> The concept of eudaimonia, a key term in ancient Greek moral philosophy ... is standardly translated as

---

[9] http://plato.stanford.edu/entries/ethics-virtue/ (accessed April 2016).

> "happiness" or "flourishing" and occasionally as "well-being."

The author goes on to explore some of the ways that each of these words captures, and does not capture, the essence of Eudaimonia. I am going to run with the word "flourish" as long as we do not understand that as mere physical survival as the article suggests may be one form of understanding. Rather, I mean flourishing in the sense of becoming fully human with respect to all the excellence of human character.

With this understanding in mind, the author considers what all is involved with "possessing" a virtue. Having a virtue, it turns out, is nothing at all like getting earrings or even learning another language. As the author describes,

> A virtue such as honesty or generosity is not just a tendency to do what is honest or generous, nor is it to be helpfully specified as a "desirable" or "morally valuable" character trait. It is, indeed a character trait – that is, a disposition which is well entrenched in its possessor, something that, as we say "goes all the way down", unlike a habit such as being a tea-drinker – but the disposition in question, far from being a single track disposition to do honest actions, or even honest actions for certain reasons, is multi-track. **It is concerned with many other actions as well, with emotions and emotional reactions, choices, values, desires, perceptions, attitudes, interests, expectations and sensibilities.** To possess a virtue is to be a certain sort of person with a certain complex mindset. (**emphasis mine**)

Notice how a virtue is not even plausibly isolated from the rest of the human mind and soul. We do not merely perform virtuous functions, nor merely think virtuous thoughts. To possess the characteristic of **being virtuous** involves our understanding of the world around us, our emotional dispositions, our will, and much more. The very foundation of our worldview, our personality and even our very soul is modified when we become virtuous.

But what if virtues were simply implanted at birth? There would be no shifting of our nature during our lifetime precisely because we already had all the virtues we required. We would be born completely virtuous. This runs into a problem too. The author describes something she calls "practical wisdom" or *phronesis*.

> Aristotle makes a number of specific remarks about phronesis that are the subject of much scholarly debate, but the (related) modern concept is best understood by thinking of **what the virtuous morally mature adult has that nice children, including nice adolescents, lack**. Both the virtuous adult and the nice child have good intentions, but the child is much more prone to mess things up **because he is ignorant of what he needs to know** in order to do what he intends. (emphasis mine)

Thus, in order for a child to be truly virtuous from the moment of their birth they must not only possess good intentions and a general understanding of what is virtuous, they must also possess sufficient understanding of the world around them and its operation in order to actualize the other ingredients of their virtuous nature. After all, the world we are looking for here is a world where nobody does anything that might "mess things up" as the author euphemistically describes it. Virtue without sufficient knowledge is likely to introduce just as much horror and vice as the author goes on to illustrate. Thus virtue, complete virtue, also requires a sufficiently detailed knowledge of the world.

Well this is all getting a lot more complicated than just slapping some virtue on every newborn and settling back into the "perfect world" that we all imagined it would be. Not only do the newborns need to be nice, they also need to be as knowledgeable as adults. In fact, even some adults I know could stand to grow a bit in this area (I include myself). In order to accomplish true virtue-from-birth every newborn would need as much "practical wisdom" as the wisest sage among us.

In other words, we need to be born old. We would need to come out of the womb fully human with no potential for growth in any area of life, not merely in the arena of virtues. Even if we could postulate perfectly fulfilled human babies with no potential in any area of life (otherwise they would not meet the complex criteria necessary for being "virtuous") this really is an entirely different kettle of fish than just imagining babies who inevitably grow up to be generally nice people.

Furthermore, it is not nearly enough for God to instill virtue at the moment of birth (as well as all the worldview, emotional, psychological, will, soul details that are necessary to sustain virtue) God would have to make sure that nobody ever changed. Not only have we now been stripped of our moral freedom, we have also been stripped of any possibility of changing our belief system, of changing our will and desires, growing in knowledge or any of the other pieces of the virtue puzzle that we need in place. All of this is necessary in order to ensure that all the humans in the "perfect world" are always, and always remain, virtuous.

In our world, however, this practical wisdom, "characteristically comes only with experience of life." Again, she is by no means speaking to the present debate, but her insight is still relevant. The only means we know of for virtue development is through life experience. She discusses this at some length.

> It is the exercise of the virtues during one's life that is held to be at least partially constitutive of eudaimonia… Given the sorts of considerations that courageous, honest, loyal, charitable people wholeheartedly recognise as reasons for action, they may find themselves compelled to face danger for a worthwhile end, to speak out in someone's defence, or refuse to reveal the names of their comrades, even when they know that this will inevitably lead to their execution, to share their last crust and face starvation. On the view that the exercise of the virtues is necessary but not sufficient for eudaimonia, such cases are described as those in which the virtuous agent sees that, as things have unfortunately turned out, eudaimonia is not possible for them (Foot 2001, 95). On the Stoical view that it is both necessary and sufficient, a eudaimon life is a life that has been successfully lived (where "success" of course is not to be understood in a materialistic way) and such people die knowing not only that they have made a success of their lives but that they have also brought their lives to a markedly successful completion. Either way, such heroic acts can hardly be regarded as egoistic.
>
> She considers two possible scenarios. First, the exercise of virtue is necessary but not sufficient for human

flourishing. Second, the exercise of virtue is necessary and sufficient for human flourishing. In both cases the **exercise of virtue is considered necessary** for human flourishing, for eudaimonia. Again, she is not attempting to address the question of whether or not human virtues could be implanted prior to any life experience, but the way she presents the subject it is terribly difficult to imagine that she would consider such a view viable.

I would suggest it is not viable. And if the concept of implanted virtue, ingrained heroism, is not a viable option, then the only alternative is a learned heroism. If learning is the only means to heroism then we need a classroom with sufficient "educational opportunities." As unpleasant as it may seem, just as boot camp may seem terribly unpleasant to the new recruit to the armed forces, this world with all of its horrors, disasters and moral outrage is precisely the venue we require to succeed as humans, "where 'success' of course is not to be understood in a materialistic way."

Objections: An Overview

To propose that this world is morally good despite the vast quantities of evil and suffering is to introduce a concept that will obviously be met with some resistance. I will consider various objections in the following chapters. I've been involved in the field of apologetics long enough to know that the quality of objections is equally distributed between two extremes, really good objections and really lousy objections. It would not be possible to consider every half-baked objection that can be levelled against the Christian worldview, not even against a specific argument like this one. The objections that follow are only a few of what I consider to be potentially the most reasonable objections. The intent is not to answer every possible objection but to illustrate how most of these objections end up being flawed when you actually spend some time thinking through them.

Before we get to those, though, consider what any objection would ultimately need to accomplish. Anybody who claims that God is a moral monster for creating this world is suggesting that God should not have created this world. Well God's options were fairly limited.

1. Create nothing.
2. Create our world.
3. Create some other world.

Pick one. I don't think most of God's critics would seriously advance the idea that God should not have created anything at all. Most of them would probably suggest that there is a different, better, world that God ought to have created. Fair enough, tell us about that world. As the previous chapter attempted to illustrate, and as I will explore further in the following chapters, the alternatives are not so obviously superior to what we have. They may be better in some ways, but they would be demonstrably worse in other ways. So if somebody doesn't like this world then what alternative would they propose? When they offer some alternative – if they even bother to offer some alternative – consider carefully all the implications and unintended consequences of their alternative (as I attempted to do in the last chapter). It seems to me that most alternative worlds are either logically impossible (like a world with free will but no possibility of moral evil) or they are logically possible but the consequences of creating such a world haven't been seriously thought through.

And if they don't have an alternative to offer, if they just like to complain, well that should tell you something.

But suppose they want to argue that God should have made the "perfect world" alternative that I described previously and which I will expound upon shortly. Despite the fact that such a world would be devoid of any virtue, any heroism, any nobility, indeed anything that gives the human experience any depth and significance, they still believe God should have created that world. It is not enough to point out that they, personally, would have preferred such a world because we can simply point out that God, personally, preferred this one. His preferences trump ours; end of conversation. It is not enough to point out that God **could** have made such a world because such declarations are trivially true and uninteresting. The only real option at their disposal is to argue that God **should** have made that world. God was morally obligated, as a morally perfect being, to create the "perfect world."

One reason it would be interesting to argue, on moral grounds, that God ought to have created this "perfect world" that I described is because a person would essentially be arguing that God was morally obligated to create a world devoid of moral obligations for anybody else. It would have been better for God to create a world without any degrees of better and worse for anybody else. We can speak of duties that God has, but he has absolutely no right to impose duties on those he creates. It would have been kinder of God to create a world where I am not expected to be kind. God should have been more compassionate so that I don't have to be! I would be very interested in seeing somebody argue on moral grounds that this world is objectively morally wrong precisely because they would be applying a measuring stick to God that they vehemently refuse to allow God to apply to them. It would be an ironic state of affairs to argue from such a perspective, but anything short of God's **moral obligation** to create the "perfect world" is mere complaining and blustering.

That all assumes, of course, that they run with the "perfect world" option that I described. Again, if they actually provide details of some other Plan B that they feel God should have created, well then you'll need to consider their proposal on its own merits.

So, as we consider various objections through these next chapters, please bear in mind that coming up with a viable alternative is really the path that any logical objection needs to end up walking. If somebody is going to complain about this world like an armchair quarterback complains about the play that the actual quarterback ran, it is never enough to say, "that was the wrong choice," demand nothing short of, "this is what should have been done, and here's why." What does the world look like that God should have created (details, please)? Please explain why God was morally obligated to create said world instead of ours?

Even if the objections to my argument succeed in undermining the moral goodness of this world, the objector is still only half way there.

Objection 1 – Too Much Suffering

Some people, such as I, propose that the suffering we see in our world may be necessary for some greater good. Others object. One of the most common objections is that there is too much suffering. Maybe some is permissible, perhaps even necessary for some good, but really?! This much?! The most obvious question to respond with is, "Then how much suffering **is** justifiable?" and of course, the equally obvious question, "How do you **know** that?" To offer absolutely nothing to the conversation except, "Well, surely **this** is too much" is to advance the conversation exactly nowhere. As I described previously, don't let people get away with complaining if they don't have a decent "plan B" to offer the conversation.

Consider what is implied when somebody says there is "too much" of something; they have some ideal or goal in mind that **requires at least some** of whatever it is we are talking about. If I put too much flour in a recipe then the cookies will taste horrible. If I use the right amount then the cookies are delicious. Too little would also be problematic. If I eat too much it is because the amount of food I consume surpasses my body's caloric needs. If I spend too much time at work then either I am not being paid enough or I have a workaholic problem.

Essentially we're talking about a Goldilocks level of suffering. The claim is made that the suffering in the world is a papa bear portion whereas it ought to be a mama bear portion. I don't know of anybody who claims we're looking at a baby bear portion.

In every case, though, whatever it is that we are saying there is "too much" of (flour, food, work, suffering) serves the purpose of being the cause of some other positive result that we seek. Flour is not something we care for on its own, we use it to make cookies. Food is certainly delightful on its own (well, not cooked vegetables!) but it also serves the important function of nourishing our bodies. Work is necessary to pay the bills, and some people definitely love their jobs, but most of us understand the importance of leisure time; that whole work-life balance thing. When we say there is "too much" of something we implicitly acknowledge that whatever it is we are talking about is serving some purpose beyond itself. Thus, as a very good starting point, those who say this world has "too much" suffering are implicitly acknowledging that suffering serves some purpose. This is precisely my point in the previous chapter that explains the need for at least some difficulty, suffering and challenges in this life. If suffering served no purpose at all then even the slightest bit of suffering would be too much; we should just get rid of it entirely! The charge of "too much" only makes sense because we agree that some good is coming from it; at least some suffering is necessary. The question then becomes whether the cause exceeds what is required for the effect. In other words, did God put too much flour in the cookie dough?

In order to answer the question of whether there is too much suffering in the world relative to the desired effect (i.e. what God wanted out of the world) we have to consider the relationship between suffering and the heroism that emerges from it (among other positive effects). In this chapter I will consider two broad questions. First, could heroism exist in the absence of any kind of challenge of any sort? Second, what does the ideal hero-building world look like? As we explore these questions the idea that there is "too much" suffering will be examined.

[While I focus on the problem of pain and suffering throughout this book, I am only touching on the problem of evil. This is because suffering was on my mind, due to life circumstances. Evil is a whole other topic but, honestly, one that I actually think is much easier to deal with. Suffering, it seems to me, is the tougher nut to crack.]

Suffering-free heroism?

Part of the complex picture of good that arises from suffering is the nobility of the human spirit that grows from the dirt of unpleasant circumstances. When a person suffers there are two ways that heroism can emerge. First, heroism is possible for the person who is suffering. Second, heroism is possible in those around the sufferer as they respond to somebody else's suffering. As I discussed previously, the very nature of suffering is such that it gives us the choice of how we are going to respond. Opportunity and choice are absolutely necessary if we are to have the freedom to choose to live heroically, virtuously. Whether we choose to act heroically when given the opportunity, well, that's up to us. All God can do is create a world with sufficient opportunity and creatures with sufficient freedom, after that the ball is in our court.

Really, is that all God could do? Could heroism (or any virtue) simply "come to be" without having been developed through choices made? Could we have great depth of character simply instilled in us so that the world could be free of any challenges, hardships, suffering, death or any kind of unpleasantness at all? What if God created us with all the ideal virtues **and** he created the world to be absolutely "perfect."

I have already touched on this subject in more depth elsewhere, so I'll just summarize briefly here. In a world devoid of any possibility of harm, nothing I do could possibly be either evil or good. Therefore, why have virtues in such a world? They would be an absolutely irrelevant feature of the human species, like having the ability to swim 100 km non-stop in a world devoid of water, or the ability to juggle in a world without gravity. Even if God instilled in us the greatest of all possible virtues, frankly we would never even know that we had such virtues if we lived in a world where nothing we did was either evil or good. The very concept of virtues would be utterly meaningless so it would be pointless for God to instill them in us in such a world.

But there is a second problem with that idea; it fails to grasp the very nature of virtue. Consider the following example. At some of the heavy traffic intersections downtown they have a special signal for blind people. When the walk signal indicates "go" then a distinct chirping sound is heard. When a blind person hears the chirping sound then they know it is safe to cross the street. This helps keep blind people safe.

Not all intersections have this feature. Suppose I see a blind person at an intersection without the chirping alarm. When the walk signal indicates, "go" I politely let them know it is safe to cross. The chirping alarm and I have both performed precisely the same function, practically speaking – a function that aids somebody else – so would it be safe to say that I and the chirping alarm are equally virtuous? Am I not morally better than some automated alarm that's plugged into the traffic light electronic system? Clearly the human decision to help another person is morally significant whereas the light signal is amoral in nature, neither good nor bad.

Where is the difference? It lies, partly, in the reality of choice. Virtues (like heroism) involve comprehension, intentionality and choice (possibly other factors too). I have to decide to do something helpful before my action is virtuous. If, however, I have been automatically endowed with such character from the moment of my birth then the option of doing something non-virtuous was never available to me. For human actions to be truly heroic the option of not doing the right thing must be a real option otherwise our "heroism" is no more authentic than the chirping signal's "heroism." If heroism could be magically bestowed upon people then having such heroism placed in our nature without our choice would turn us into "hero robots" who simply act without choosing. But that is not true heroism. Because we have to sincerely choose between two alternatives without having the outcome of our choice predetermined for us by some implanted hero-nature, heroism and virtue are only possible through the choices we make in the life circumstances we face. Virtue cannot be installed at start-up, so to speak. Just as it is logically impossible to force love, it is equally logically impossible to impose virtue.

And if it is not logically possible for humans to be endowed with heroism prior to making heroic choices then not even God could accomplish such a feat. After all, Omnipotence entails the ability to do what is **logically possible**.[10] If "instilled heroism" is logically impossible then not even almighty God can make it happen.

Thus a world devoid of any kind of difficulty, hardship or challenge (a "perfect world") that is also packed with heroes, is a logically impossible world. The first option is not available to us; there must be some difficulty that we need to deal with. But the question is, how much suffering is "sufficient" as I mentioned earlier? Surely this world has gone overboard! This leads us to our second general question, could the same magnitude of heroism emerge with less suffering? To answer this, we must consider the ideal hero-building world.

The ideal hero-building world

Why this world? Couldn't the entire hero-building enterprise unfold in a better world? Let's imagine altering our present world through a substantial reduction in suffering on the one hand, and a substantial increase on the other hand. What effects would those have on the heroism of our world?

Suppose, for instance, that only one human every year contracted a deadly disease. Just a single human out of the entire human race. That sounds like a much better world already, doesn't it? But what effect might that have on human heroism? Well, a few obvious observations. There would probably be other people who would respond by helping that poor soul but how many would? For instance, if there was only one sick person

---

[10] A lot of people, even Christians, misunderstand the meaning of the term "omnipotence." It does not involve the ability to make four-sided triangles, for instance.
   Here are two articles that cover this subject in some depth:
http://christianthinktank.com/notsobig.html and
http://plato.stanford.edu/entries/omnipotence/ (accessed April 2016).

per year, and this year the person was in the remote recesses of Uzbekistan, what can I possibly do to help them? Even if I wanted to, I am powerless because they live so ridiculously far away from me. It would not be wise of me to go and try to help them. Just imagine if every person on the planet boarded a plane the moment the opportunity to help the sick person became publically known. Uzbekistan would be bursting at the seams; too many cooks in the kitchen! While a single person suffers, the vast majority of the billions of people on the planet are, practically speaking, completely helpless to do anything. For the vast majority of people on the planet there would be no opportunity for heroism.

But there is another problem with such a world: would we even know what to do to help them? With an almost total lack of suffering and hardship in our everyday lives we would have no context for understanding how we could help when the opportunity arose. We would have no experience, nor would those around us have any knowledge of what to do. Role models and our own practice make us proficient at helping others; in a world with too little suffering we would have neither. The less suffering there is, the fewer opportunities to practice and therefore the less equipped we are to deal with suffering when it does cross our paths. We need to live in a world with a fairly frequent occurrence of suffering in order to be properly skilled, at a moment's notice, to do something about it. Even if I, personally, am not skilled in all these areas, humanity needs to collectively have some idea of what to do. Even in Uzbekistan.

Now of course one diseased person per year is remarkably low. What about two? Still too low. Even if we had dozens, or hundreds of diseased people each year we, as a human race, would not develop the skills to engage such hardship in any meaningful way. Thus we find that there is a line somewhere (I am not going to venture a guess as to where that line exactly is) below which suffering and hardship would be so infrequent as to render us unable to collectively learn how to deal with it. In that situation any attempts at heroism would almost certainly fail and despair would be the order of the day instead of hope. Despair and, of course, apathy. The guy is in Uzbekistan, what can I do? Shrug shoulders and move on. There can be no heroism if our reaction is "we have no idea what to do here…" and "Where in the world is Uzbekistan?"

In a world with too little suffering the potential for heroism would be diminished along with the suffering; this would result in a world where suffering would not accomplish its purpose. So too little suffering turns out to be counterproductive, but what about an increase in suffering? Would a world with greater hardship end up giving us greater opportunity for heroism? Perhaps, but even that conceptual world finds an upper limit in its hero-building potential. If every human were stricken with cancer simultaneously, for instance, then there would be no healthy humans to heroically aid those who were dying. That may provide plenty of opportunities for heroism to that one generation but there would be no subsequent generations of heroes. Thus ends the entire system; not so good after all.

What we need is a world where most of humanity is not enduring great personal hardship at any given moment (their time will come…) so that they are able to provide a stable base for indirect heroism in the lives of those who are. Through the work of the many, society can continue and progress while the few are facing their own personal hardship. There should always be more civilians than soldiers, for instance. There should be more doctors and nurses than patients. There should be more people who have their limbs than those who have lost them. We need more peace than war, more loving parents than abusive ones, more lovers than rapists, more natural deaths than murders and so on. Not surprisingly, this is the world we find ourselves in. If the pendulum swings too far toward disaster then the stability – even the very existence – of humanity is threatened. And if the pendulum swings too far toward lack of disaster then heroism dies a rapid death.

The ideal hero-building world should provide every human with multiple opportunities for heroism during their lifetime, though the demand for heroism within the human race as a whole needs to be sufficiently rare so we can get on with "living life" between those heroic moments.

Too little suffering would yield despair because we wouldn't know how to help. Too much suffering would yield despair because anything we did would be pointless. In the middle is that "sweet spot" where heroism can flourish because it can still be grounded in a general attitude of hope across humanity. Our present world avoids those two extremes and is somewhere near the "sweet spot" where hope is the grounding of successful heroism.

The world needs to look something like our world in order to succeed in raising up the greatest number and quality of heroes. When confronted with evil and suffering in our world perhaps we should spend less time asking, "Could God have done away with this particular situation?" and start asking, "What am I going to do about this particular situation?" In other words, start acting heroically. God created a world with such opportunities, what are you going to do about it?

Gratuitous Evil and Suffering

I wanted to end with some thoughts on the claim that some instances of evil and suffering are gratuitous. This is a common charge. Consider what the word "gratuitous" means. I'm pretty sure the definition that's in mind when it is used in this context is, "Being without apparent reason, cause, or justification."[11]

The concept appears to be that some evil or suffering might be justifiable, but there is just too much of it and there is no reason for certain instances or varieties of it. If my theory is right regarding the relationship between moral freedom and the hardships of this world on the one hand, and character development (i.e. hero-building) on the other hand, then it is hard to see how any evil or suffering could be gratuitous, by definition.

Even though I am not addressing evil directly in this book (as mentioned earlier), I'll briefly touch on it here. What people often forget is that evil is not a thing. Evil is a choice that a person made: a morally bad, non-virtuous,/ non-heroic choice. Speaking of the "evil in the world" is to fundamentally misunderstand the issue. It would be more accurate to describe it as the "evil choices that humans make in the world." The root problem is not the evil – as if evil were some cosmic blob of substance – but the fact that humans choose to introduce said evil into the world. Evil, after all, does not magically spring into being out of nothing; it has a cause and **we are its cause**.

However, as I described previously, evil is only possible in a world with moral freedom and it is this same moral freedom that allows us the opportunity to become people of great virtue. When considering evil, then I would grant that every single instance of evil is unnecessary, unjustified! In one sense it's all gratuitous. But that's not the fundamental issue, what we need to think about is moral freedom. The question to ask is whether there is gratuitous moral freedom. Do we have more freedom than we ought to? Should God have reduced everybody's freedom? Should some humans not have any moral freedom? That might sound like a good idea until (as is a common theme in this book) we consider the unintended consequences of limited human freedom. If we start stripping people of their moral freedom, well I think it should be apparent what kind of pickle we will get ourselves into. Where do we draw the line? What other consequences might there be to such a world? Again, if somebody thinks that's how God should have created the world, get them to describe it in some detail and see if such a world is either logically possible or qualitatively better than ours.

What about suffering? Is some of it gratuitous? Moral freedom provides the opportunity for the development of character by choosing good over evil (an opportunity which can obviously be eschewed) and suffering also provides the opportunity for development of character by choosing to

---

[11] Gratuitous: Dictionary.com, Random House, http://www.dictionary.com/browse/gratuitous (accessed April 2016).

respond heroically (which, once again, can be eschewed). The only circumstance under which suffering could theoretically be gratuitous is if there was not even the possibility that any character development, any heroism, could arise as a result of the suffering. Even when we hear about some horrific suffering in somebody else's life, a suffering that hypothetically offered them no opportunity to respond heroically, the moment we end up talking about it and dissecting it we have the opportunity to act heroically by helping prevent those in the future or preparing for the next instance. Indeed, the moment any human is consciously aware of any instance of suffering the potential for heroism is immediately present. Thus the only instances of suffering that could, even in theory, be absolutely gratuitous would be instances that no human was aware of, by definition; not even the human that is enduring the suffering. But if we don't know about them, how can we know such gratuitous suffering exists? We are speculating at that point.[12]

Certainly we can think of many, many, instances of suffering where nobody became a better person because of it (some people descend into bitterness, self-pity or maybe hatred of the world) but the problem is not with the suffering, it is with the person's response to it. As with moral freedom, if we start eliminating those instances of choice where we know the opportunity is not going to be seized, there are unintended consequences which are often not considered carefully.

There is another side of the whole "gratuitous suffering" discussion that does not sit well with me either. When people get all up in arms about some of the suffering in the world and they call it "gratuitous," what that says to me is that they are quite content to let some of the suffering remain. It seems to me that there is something horribly wrong with a person who is "content" with a certain amount of suffering after they have gotten rid of the really bad stuff. It would be like somebody demanding that God should have prevented some disease in a child, but they say nothing about diseases in adults. Would this person, if they became a doctor, only work to get rid of childhood diseases and just leave the adults to die? Are humans disposable once they have reached the age of eighteen? Forty? Sixty? Eighty? How did you decide the age of expendability, anyway? How inhumane is that! There are documented examples in history of societies who have decided that certain demographics are worth protecting and other demographics are expendable. I don't think I need to tell you how horrific the results are of such types of thinking.

If we believe that some suffering is gratuitous and some is not, and if

---

[12] I can already see skeptics jumping all over animal suffering prior to humanity – I'll take a closer look at that later.

God were to eliminate the gratuitous suffering then it naturally follows that humans would be less concerned with the suffering that remained. After all, it is justifiable. It would become far too easy to shrug it off.

It seems to me that the right approach is to recognize that none of the suffering in our world is gratuitous at all, and all of it, absolutely every instance of it, deserves our attention as we work to alleviate it. We should never embrace suffering nor excuse it, but take it seriously and work hard to alleviate it whenever and wherever we are able. Placing it on a scale and deciding what's in and what's out seems to me just about as heartless a thing as any human can do. It gives us grounds to ignore the suffering of some people because, "Oh, well, at least she wasn't a child" or "Hey, that just happens in our world." The last thing I would want to do is shrug off another human being simply because their suffering didn't happen to fit into my subjective definition of gratuitous. Some people complain that God should not have allowed children to die of cancer but when my grandmother died I can assure that was devastating for me. She was not expendable, even at eighty. She was still fully human, no more and no less so than a child.

It seems to me that we ought to deal with evil and suffering as package deals instead of dividing them up into evils that we will allow, suffering we are willing to put up with and those that are "gratuitous." Either God has sufficient reason for allowing evil and suffering (of all magnitudes) or he does not. Our duty, though, is to combat all of it instead of finding grounds to shirk our heroic responsibilities in some cases.

Objection 2 – Suffering Is Unfairly Distributed

In this chapter I want to consider the uneven distribution of evil and suffering and the unfair distribution of evil and suffering; two distinct challenges. Some places and people have it worse than others, what are we to make of that?

Suffering should be evenly distributed

It would make more sense, would it not, if the suffering in the world were more equally distributed? Why is there more suffering in less developed nations than in more developed nations, for instance? Why do some parts of the world seem prone to natural disasters and other parts seem relatively safe? Couldn't God have spread the suffering around a little better; a little less "lumpy?" If suffering is a logically necessary ingredient for authentic heroism we should expect it everywhere in roughly equivalent proportions. If we cannot eliminate it (because it serves a necessary role in the betterment of our character) then at least the world should avoid unusually high concentrations of suffering while others live in relative comfort.

While part of the disparity of suffering is human caused, like when warlords hoard all the food for themselves during a famine and refuse to share with the starving masses, the lack of equality in other forms of suffering has nothing to do with human choice. No mountain village, for instance, will ever experience a tsunami. Siberia has never suffered under a tropical storm or a hurricane. Some diseases are quite localized.

When considering this objection my first observation would be to point out that any given form of suffering may not be perfectly uniformly distributed, but suffering on the whole seems to be sufficiently evenly distributed. We will all face it someday. Siberia may never have endured a hurricane like a Caribbean island, but it should also be pointed out that the Caribbean islands have never endured a Siberian winter. Though some diseases may be relatively localized to one area, other diseases may be more localized to another area. Diseases, overall, plague the entire planet; nobody is safe. Frankly, it would be difficult to find any place on earth that is absolutely devoid of any natural disasters, diseases or hardships of any kinds. There may be substantially more hardships in some places and less in others but one way or another we are all faced with these challenges in life.

One needs to consider what life would be like if suffering were perfectly evenly distributed. If hurricanes struck everywhere and every disease was perfectly randomly distributed across the planet, would that be better? Not really. We suffer in the present world and we would still suffer in that hypothetical world. The challenge that suffering presents to humanity, and the resultant opportunities for heroism that suffering entails, would still be perfectly accessible to all humans, just as they are now. How is that an improvement on the current state of affairs? I'm not convinced it is. In fact it might make things worse if everybody were sick, as discussed previously.

Furthermore, the inequality in the distribution of suffering as it exists in our present world does offer various other opportunities for heroism that would be lost if all hardships were perfectly evenly distributed. For instance, the doctor who gives up the familiarity of his home town and relocates his family to another part of the world in order to battle a disease that only exists in that part of the world exhibits a depth of character that exceeds another doctor who battles only those diseases that are in his own back yard. Both doctors are obviously heroic, but the doctor who chooses to fight remote diseases exhibits a different form (or magnitude) of heroism. Such exceptional displays of self-sacrifice would be impossible if suffering were perfectly uniformly distributed across the globe because every disease would be in every doctor's back yard.

Not only does the uneven distribution of certain forms of suffering provide the opportunity for novel forms of heroism, in some cases it makes heroism possible at all. To dovetail off of an idea that I introduced previously (colossal suffering for everybody) consider how psychotic dictators have made a real mess of some of the worst nations in the world. Through their abysmal "leadership," industry is made substantially more difficult. Is it any surprise that such nations are not at the leading edge of scientific and medical research? However, when the actions of the dictator produce results within their nation that require the benefit of advances in scientific and medical research, who do they call? Naturally they have to talk to other nations without dictators where the real advancement of science and medicine take place. But, to get back to our point about an equal distribution of suffering, if every nation were governed by psychotic dictators then no nation would have the scientific or medical research to help any other nation, let alone the citizens within their own borders. It is the imperfect distribution of certain forms of evil and suffering that makes it possible for humans to heroically respond to instances of evil and suffering that they are not personally enduring. We need nations without dictators if there is going to be the infrastructure necessary to help those nations with dictators.

In other words, often humanity can respond to horrors in one place, time and people group precisely because those in another place, time and people group are not experiencing those horrors. The somewhat uneven distribution of certain kinds of evil and suffering makes certain kinds of heroism possible in the first place.

Suffering should be fairly distributed

It is one thing to claim that suffering should be evenly distributed and another thing to claim that suffering should be fairly distributed. In other words, those who deserve to suffer ought to suffer, but not the rest of us. Interestingly, one cannot really ask for both. If somebody says they think suffering should be perfectly evenly distributed **and** they think suffering should be perfectly fairly distributed, point out that those two requests actually run counter to each other. Unless they believe every human being is morally equivalent (Hitler was on par with Martin Luther King Jr.) then a "fair" distribution of suffering would be anything but equal!

I digress. Any kind of "character dependent" distribution of suffering would undermine the fundamental purpose of heroism. One necessary condition to being a real hero is to respond to a situation in the morally right way with no regard to any personal benefits. If, on the other hand, it was well known that those who "live right" are supernaturally protected from a wide array of hardships, then people's motivation for heroism would be selfish, not selfless. Suppose, for instance, that scientists discovered that as long as a person is a registered and active volunteer firefighter, that person would never contract cancer. If no volunteer firefighter ever got cancer, the very next day there would be a line-up of volunteers eager to sign up at the fire station; the line would extend around the block! What would motivate the new volunteers? Heroism? Absolutely not! Self-interest and self-preservation would be the underlying motives. Faux heroism would rule the day if suffering were only experienced by those who deserved it.

Even Christian theology is nuanced enough to account for this; Salvation for the next life is not dependent on our works and good behaviour in this life, it is understood to be an unmerited gift. Hitler and

MLK both had equal access to God's grace, but we get the strong sense that Hitler declined the offer. Even so, the offer was legitimately extended by God, regardless of his past errors. If God's grace were based on our "good lives" then the New Earth would be packed full of frauds. Authentic heroism is never motivated by self-interest.

There is another aspect of Christian theology that comes to mind on this subject and that is Jesus' comment that "he who is without sin should cast the first stone." (John 8:7) Perhaps those who wish that suffering would only befall those who deserved it might consider carefully just who it is who gets to decide which humans deserve suffering and which do not. There is no wisdom in the human who appeals to the justice of God; there is great wisdom in appealing to his mercy.

Furthermore, if suffering only struck those who deserved it, why should I help them? Our moral intuitions would kick in and we would more readily ignore the suffering of others; they had it coming! The entire motivation for heroism in the face of suffering is precisely that this person does not deserve to suffer, or at least they do not deserve it any more than any other person (to follow the Christian paradigm). That inherent lack of "justice" is precisely the thing that we are being called to correct through our heroic actions. We already know that God will balance the scales of justice one day, the really interesting question is whether or not you and I are going to do anything about it today.

[An obvious exception to all this would be situations were a person's suffering is self-inflicted. One has little pity for the man who stuffs his face with Twinkies and never lifts a finger, then complains to God when he has heart problems and dies in his fifties because he's 200 pounds overweight. Obviously we should still help the man, if he is open to being helped, but we intuitively realize that blaming God in such circumstances is a rather laughable charge.]

What about the youth? Surely they do not deserve to suffer. That is an interesting idea but let me ask this, what should the cut-off age be? Seven? Twelve? Eighteen? Whatever the age is, can we even begin to fathom the horror that would be associated with growing up? If diseases, disfigurements, natural disasters, accidents and so on would never strike anybody under the age of eighteen – if the youth were truly invincible – how terrifying would life be for all the seventeen-year-olds? Would a person's eighteenth birthday be a time of celebration or a time to hide in the basement and not come out? Indeed, such "special treatment" would introduce a whole new level of psychological terror for those just prior to the arbitrary cut-off age. The likelihood is still there that they would end up facing life's hardships just like the rest of us; they would merely postpone it.

So they still suffer, just like in this world, but now there is the added influence of immense psychological trauma when they reach the age of "maturity."

There would also be an added problematic dimension to a world like that. Part of the purpose of getting bumps and bruises as children is to prepare us for the world around us. If in the first eighteen years of our lives we never got sick, never broke a bone and could not possibly die, then we would acquire eighteen years of invincibility-induced bad habits that would put us at extra risk when we passed that particular milestone. This, it seems to me, would greatly increase the likelihood of suffering and death among eighteen-year-olds as they emerged from their arbitrary protective "bubble" and came face-to-face with reality.

My wife's cardiac arrest occurred when she was in her mid-thirties. Every time she visited the cardiologist, before and after the incident, she was always the youngest in the waiting room. She isn't supposed to have these kinds of problems at her age. Even so, are the rest of the people in the waiting room expendable? I think not! That's somebody else's wife. That's somebody's uncle. That's somebody's grandma. These other humans, though of a different "vintage" than Denise, are fully human, fully valuable and completely worth saving.

I fail to see how singling out the young for protection is an improvement. The loss of infants and children is tragic, absolutely, but they are human just like the rest of us. The loss of any human is tragic; let's not start playing favourites.

Summary

I argued that suffering must be sufficiently evenly distributed in order to provide everybody the opportunity for heroism (either through personal suffering or to intervene in the suffering of others) and I also argued that it must be more or less random to ensure that one's motives for heroism are pure; they are truly heroic. Young, old, innocent, guilty, male, female, black, white; we all suffer in various ways and it has nothing at all to do with what we have done or not done in this life. It is not warranted suffering.

Thus we find that suffering needs to be sufficiently evenly distributed, but there are benefits to a less-than-perfectly-even distribution of suffering. We also find that suffering should be "no respecter of persons," it could happen to anybody at any time. It seems to me that such an equation is necessary to maximize the possibility of human flourishing vis-à-vis heroism.

Not surprisingly, this is more or less what our world looks like. Since this world provides the opportunity to maximize our heroism the question that needs asking, as always, is "what are you going to do about it?" Is your "hero within" going to emerge into the world and make a real difference?

Objection 3 – Why Me?

Even if we acknowledge that the difficulties of this life are the only means by which we can become the best kind of people God gave us the potential to become, that still does not give us a lot of comfort as we "walk through the valley of the shadow of death." What are we to make of these difficult situations from a more personal level? Even if suffering is necessary, when it is our turn we still ask, "Why me?"

Why me?

As far as we know Denise was born with a heart that doesn't work quite right.[13] Since before we were married she has had a cardiologist, been subjected to countless tests, and had to take an ever-increasing number of pills each day. And we always knew she was at risk of exactly what happened on April 16, 2013. Have we had some conversations around the question of "why me?" I can assure you we have had our fair share.

This is absolutely the most natural and expected question that a person could ask when something horrible happens to them. Part of the reason it is impossible to answer most of the time (barring those occasions of self-inflicted suffering) is because, though it is the most natural of questions, it is also fundamentally the wrong question.

Consider the assumptions behind the question. First of all, the questioner is asking for a reason, a purpose, a motivation behind the suffering. That is the essence of the "why" part of the question. But they are not asking "why" in a generic sense. A person who asks "Why me?" is

---

[13] For those with a medical background, Denise has an enlarged left ventricle, low ejection fraction and a "regularly irregular" heartbeat, namely cardiomyopathy.

not asking "Why does suffering exist?" That would be a question with a generic, universal answer; they are looking for a specific, personal answer. The assumption behind the question is that there is a meaning to their suffering in particular and that meaning relates to them specifically. Perhaps it is justice for some previous moral infraction (i.e. if the world were governed by karma and reincarnation).[14] Perhaps their suffering will make the rest of their life better than it would otherwise have been, like how the unpleasantness of a needle may cure them of a disease. Perhaps they are specifically being made to suffer for the betterment of humanity; a role very few people have sufficient nobility to accept, even if they were to be made aware of it.

But what if your specific situation isn't about you? You didn't do something wrong that deserved this particular circumstance. You are not paying for previous sins. You are not being made to suffer because of the sins of your parents. Some people misread Bible passages like Exodus 20:5 which seems to suggest that; a good commentary will explain why that is a misreading, and even Ezekiel 18 sets the record straight. Jesus also renounces this paradigm when speaking of the blind man by the pool waiting for healing (John 9:1–3).

Individuals suffer primarily because they are part of a system that includes, as one of its characteristics, various kinds of unpleasantness. That unpleasantness is relatively randomly distributed so specific instances of suffering do not typically carry an individual custom-made purpose but rather suffering, as a whole, is purposeful.

Regardless of the assumed reason for suffering that may be behind the question, "why me?" there is also an assumed passivity on the part of the sufferer. The suffering and its effects are assumed to be beyond their control. If something bad happens because of past infractions, well, what's done is done so there isn't much I can do about it now. If it happened because of something bad that somebody else did then, again, there is absolutely nothing that I can do about that at this point. [This was the thinking of the Israelites in exile that Ezekiel 18 is meant to address.] If I am enduring this suffering so that some glorious state of future bliss can be enjoyed, then I just have to sit back and wait it out. In all of these cases there is a mindset that assumes I have no involvement in the process. The cause is out of my control because it is in the past, or the suffering is, itself, the cause of some inevitable and much better future; I do not need to do

---

[14] In the original article I referenced another article I wrote on "yogic" religions. Yogic religions believe in karma and reincarnation which necessarily entails that any suffering a person endures in this life is a direct result of their moral infractions from the previous life.

anything. The assumption seems to be that cosmic forces beyond my control are at work and I am merely a pawn in this game.

It is perfectly normal to bemoan one's circumstances, indeed it would be odd if a person were not bothered by their own suffering. One needs to fully come to grips with the challenge they are facing before action can be taken, so asking, "why me?" is an unavoidable part of the process. But it is a process, not a bus stop. We must move past that question. It makes sense to start with asking, "why me?" but it is tragic if that is where we stop.

Contra such a passive attitude, we need to eventually ask, "What am I going to do about this?" Even if there is not a specific purpose to your specific suffering, there is a general purpose for suffering and that is to provide opportunities for heroism. If you had not fallen victim to this particular suffering you would eventually have to face some other form of suffering at some other time in your life. Given the general purpose for suffering you now have a specific opportunity because of the specific suffering you are experiencing. You almost certainly will experience even more suffering in your life once this situation is in your past. Will you walk through that open door before you, right here and right now, and grow in your nobility? Do you have (or will your grow) enough honour to help those facing such difficulties? A passive approach to suffering asks "why me?" whereas an active approach to suffering asks, "what can I do?" God is hoping people will eventually ask the second question instead of getting stuck on the first.

Why did God do this?

Again, this is fundamentally the wrong question to ask, though it is a perfectly natural impulse. God providentially set up a system that includes various challenges and also included the potential for things to devolve to our present level of suffering and evil. But it is not as though he dictates, guides or micromanages every single instance of suffering. It may seem like splitting hairs to say that God allows, or even indirectly "causes," hardship and suffering in general but that he does not allow or cause specific instances. God created a world that included birds that defecate in random locations, but it would be misguided to complain that God caused that particular bird to defecate on my particular car. When somebody builds a sports stadium the intent is that people will fill the stands, but they do not have specific seats in mind for specific people. Similarly, God created a world within which the human body may occasionally break down, but God probably did not go out of his way to ensure that my wife was born with a faulty heart. He also probably did not go out of his way to place you in your difficult circumstances whatever they may be.

[I keep qualifying the above examples with the word "probably" because there are almost certainly exceptions to this rule – God may introduce suffering that would not have otherwise happened, or alleviate suffering that would have gone on for some time on its own – but I believe these exceptions are rare and they need to be. If God intervened regularly then the category of hardship would be practically eliminated and, therefore, so would the possibility of human flourishing. Exceptions are possible, so long as they do not become the new rule. It seems wisest to me to assume that God has not micromanaged your particular situation.]

Rather, the only question we have a hope of meaningfully answering is why God allows suffering in general, which I have tried to answer, at least in part. It would be presumptuous to think we could have a full and exhaustive answer, but surely we can seek some general insights; I believe we have access to them. To seek a divine purpose for specific instances of suffering, or to ask why God did not prevent a specific instance of suffering, is the wrong question to ask.

While the general answer to why God created a world with hardship may be philosophically sound, it is often far from satisfying. It takes very little poking around the internet to find stories of people whose lives are in ruins because they run into problem after problem after problem. Atheists in particular love to bring up these stories and wallow in their horror. In some cases a person's problems are self-inflicted so, in one sense, God can hardly be blamed. Even so, if the purpose of this life is to offer us the opportunity to become heroes, if we make a mess of things wouldn't it be nice if God actually helped us out a bit and nudged us in the right direction? Why allow us to utterly destroy ourselves?

But there are others who suffer and suffer and suffer through no fault of their own. It may make sense to allow humanity to suffer in general, but surely that suffering should come in smaller doses. When we read about people who endure one hardship only to fall victim to a second hardship which is quickly followed up by yet another hardship until their families are torn apart, they become a shell of a person and they spend the rest of their lives just trying to pick up the pieces, asking "where is God?" is certainly an impulse that I feel. Let us suffer so we can grow – I get that – but why allow the suffering to pile higher and higher until there is no possibility of growth at all, just mere survival until we curl up and die? Would we not expect a loving God who wanted his creation to develop in their nobility to step in and make sure the challenges were accomplishing what they were supposed to? When they reach a point of simply destroying a person's soul – when the hardship surpasses anything that your average human could possibly grow from – why allow that? It hardly seems comforting to say that God mourns with us when the suffering is no longer productive.

I have no answers, only anecdotes of hope. Even if I cannot answer this question to my own satisfaction (much less anybody else's satisfaction) I have one small consolation; some people in those circumstances do manage to turn them around. Though many people may collapse under the weight, and nobody could possibly fault them for that, even in these horrors that stagger the imagination there are a handful of glorious instances of people who have conquered the horror; victory instead of defeat.[15]

Some research

I poked around a little bit on Google Scholar and I found a few articles with some interesting observations about the positive effects of suffering; specifically altruism. The idea seems to be that certain forms of character growth are regularly seen as a result of suffering and, in some cases, the magnitude of character growth is demonstrably higher among those who have suffered than among those who have not.

I discovered a fascinating article[16] that explores the relationship between suffering and altruism, and the relatively recently identified phenomenon of "altruism born of suffering" (ABS – no longer just a nice feature to have in your car!). The idea here is that the negative outcomes of suffering, such as Post Traumatic Stress Disorder (PTSD) tend to be the focus of a lot of attention, but those effects are far from the whole story.

> In actuality, however, only a relatively small percentage of those who have had traumatic experiences develop PTSD or other severe symptoms of trauma ... Moreover, theory and research also has come to focus on resilience after trauma, and on **posttraumatic growth** (PTG). This literature also mentions **empathy and altruism** as potential growth outcomes. **(emphasis mine)**

In other words, the literature seems to suggest that most people who endure profound suffering, though they are obviously traumatized, exhibit

---

[15] One popular example to consider is Nick Vujicic. Here's the official website for "Life Without Limbs," http://www.lifewithoutlimbs.org/ (accessed April 2016).

[16] Ervin Staub (PhD) and Johanna Vollhardt (MA), "Altruism Born of Suffering: The Roots of Caring and Helping After Victimization and Other Trauma," University of Massachusetts at Amherst, http://people.umass.edu/estaub/Altriusm%20born%20ofsuffering%20staub.pdf (accessed April 2016).

responses that reveal that their trauma is not the entire picture. After the initial trauma, there can be "growth" as well as "empathy and altruism." Or, put another way, some people become better because of their suffering; the kind of people they would not have been if they had never suffered. That personal growth did not occur without some effort on their part as I will touch on in a moment. The field is apparently a relatively new one, and results are not always consistent, but apparently the general finding is, "…the majority of individuals who have experienced stressful life events report positive changes…" Again, it is a mixed bag, as the article explains. Without stealing their thunder, here are a few snippets of research they describe:

> Among a sample of 100 Holocaust survivors, 82% reported that they had helped other prisoners in concentration camps. They reported sharing food and clothing and providing emotional support, a large majority describing their motive as altruistic.
>
> High levels of altruism and prosocial behavior have also been documented at times of natural disasters. Some scholars have written about the emergence of an "altruistic community" in the aftermath of hurricanes, floods, or earthquakes, characterized by "higher than usual levels of solidarity, fellowship, and altruism"
>
> In a correlational, cross-sectional study, undergraduate students in the United States were asked about their own past victimization and suffering. Those who reported that they had suffered from interpersonal violence, group-based violence, or a natural disaster reported significantly more feelings of empathy for, as well as personal responsibility to help victims of the Tsunami in South East Asia than a control group of students who reported no such suffering … They also volunteered to help more, by signing up to join a Tsunami relief group and collect money.

In general, the researchers summarize, "… greater physical harm, material loss, and perceived life threat were associated with providing more tangible and informational support…" In other words, the relationship between hardship and heroism is generally proportional; The greatest heroism is often exhibited by those who have endured the greatest hardship. Surprise, surprise! What ingredients tend to lead to these positive results? As the article describes (with a nice flow chart I might add) there are a number of factors but the biggest ones seem to be assistance received from others and one's own personal initiative. As I have been describing all along, part of God's purpose for suffering is for the heroism opportunities it affords the one who is suffering, but also for the heroism opportunities it affords those around them. This research suggests that if both opportunities are seized upon, then personal growth as a result of suffering is a much more frequent outcome.

The study is careful to note the limitations on their data, stating, "These findings are correlational, and we cannot exclude the possibility that they are expressions **of personal characteristics**, such as greater sensitivity to stressful events and greater dispositional empathy, **rather than suffering leading to more caring**." In other words, the suffering itself may not be the sufficient cause of these examples of altruism; something about the person's character may be involved. This goes back to my observations at the beginning of this article. Asking "why me?" implies a passive attitude whereas, "how am I going to respond?" demonstrates personal initiative. Suffering on its own cannot be expected to produce positive effects, the magic ingredient has always been the nobility of the human spirit.

I cannot help but once again use the imagery of a plant and the dirt. A seed that never gets dirty also never becomes a flower. In a similar sense, we need the suffering of life for our greatest heroic potential to blossom. But not every seed that is planted flourishes.[17] Not all of us will become the people God hopes we will choose to be as we endure suffering. But until we are buried in the dirt of suffering we will never know whether we had it in us to grow from the unpleasant circumstances in life.

In another article[18] exploring some of the effects of torture on a person, it claims that, "Many have begun to recover from torture with the help of spiritual and religious practices, work, and altruistic activities that benefit their family and community." In other words, while altruism may be an effect of some forms of suffering, altruism may be part of the road to recovery from other forms of suffering. Or, if you act like a hero then you become a hero. Once again, virtue is a result of life – particularly the

---

[17] This may sound vaguely similar to the parable of the sower of seeds in Mark 4:3–8.

[18] Richard F. Mollica, MD, "Surviving Torture," published in the *New England Journal of Medicine*, 351:1; July 1, 2004; http://healtorture.org/content/surviving-torture (accessed April 2016).

suffering we experience in life – not something that could be implanted in us without any effort on our part.

So when we ask, "Why me?" and "Why is God allowing this?" hopefully part of the answer is becoming more obvious. God almost certainly did not inflict this particular instance of suffering on you, personally. Rather, God allows suffering in general to exist so that you, and those around you, will have the opportunity to rise to the occasion, exhibit and develop altruism, and work toward post traumatic growth. In other words, so you have the chance to become a better person, the person God intended you to be. A hero. That obviously does not explain every single instance of suffering, but it seems to be a plausible reason for most types of suffering. And research suggests the desired effect is often realized, even in cases of suffering so horrific that most of us cannot fathom it.

But those positive effects will only be realized if we move beyond the question, "why doesn't God do something about this?" and start asking, "what am I going to do about this?" Do you have such nobility? This is something you need to think about because, like it or not, suffering is a feature of reality that we all need to contend with. If you haven't suffered yet, your time will almost certainly come one day.

Our family suffered in the spring of 2013, but I am not naïve enough to think that is the end of it for us. I don't know what will happen next, or who it will involve (maybe not Denise next time), but I live life a little different now that I understand that suffering is something that cannot be escaped in this life. It will happen and when it does I have the opportunity to grow, to more closely resemble God's template for my life. A template modelled by Jesus himself.

Objection 4 – The Garden of Eden and Heaven

If one needs evil and suffering in a morally good world then what are we to make of Heaven? After all, won't evil and suffering cease to exist? Furthermore, wasn't the Garden of Eden fundamentally free of suffering?

Did Eden even exist?

First things first: did Eden exist? Here is where we open the Pandora's box of the creation-evolution controversy. Thousands of pages of ink (and millions of electrons on blogger sites) get spilt annually over this subject, and the state of mass confusion on the issue within Christianity makes it most presumptuous to suppose that I can answer the question. But I don't actually think that I need to; for the sake of this discussion it doesn't matter whether Eden existed or not. I am certain that sounds like the ultimate cop-out, but work with me here.

Broadly speaking we have two options. Either Eden existed or it did not. Suppose it existed. Well, that makes things relatively easy for the sake of this discussion. We might squabble about how much of the first few chapters of Genesis represent actual events in space-time history and how much may have taken on a mythical flavour over the centuries, but we can presumably trust that the Genesis account of Eden is, by and large, theologically reliable. Through the book of Genesis we have some glimpse into a world none of us have ever experienced; the home that God created for the first humans.

What if it did not exist? I will admit that this perspective is not one I lean toward, but smarter (and for all I know, "holier") Christians than I hold to this position and I have no reason to think they are nutcases or heretics. The general idea, as far as I understand it, is that God may have introduced the story of the Garden of Eden not as an account of space-time history, but rather as a frame of reference that would inform the Israelite nation of their place in the world, the nature of God, the nature of humanity, and so on. The theory, as I understand it, is that the ancient Israelites never would have understood the Eden story as factual history in the first place, and our reading of it as such would have been laughable to them. The story of Eden, therefore, may have been Jesus' very first parable, in a manner of speaking. Not all theologians who accept the mythical flavour of Genesis 2 to 3 go as far as this, but I am considering the extremes here, for sake of argument.

[If I am not representing this view properly, my apologies, but that is my best understanding of it. I do not hold to this view but I want to do it justice nonetheless.]

What that means for our discussion, though, is that the story of Eden (assuming it is a theologically reliable parable) gives us an idea of God's understanding of a "perfect world" even if it never existed in space-time history. **God's concept of the "perfect world" is all we really need for this discussion**. If we can compare God's idea of a "perfect world" to the idea held by many humans – pure bliss, no pain, all pleasure and no work or challenges of any kind – then we can see how closely the two line up. Whether God actually created Eden, then, is less important than God's mental concept of Eden. If Eden existed then we can understand God's concept of a perfect world by looking at what he created; we can probe Genesis 2 to 3. If Eden did not exist, we can still probe Genesis 2 to 3 for insights into God's concept of a perfect world even though it remains his mental concept instead of his creation. Either way we can actually skip the entire creation-evolution discussion entirely which is kind of nice because it usually generates far more heat than light. All we care about is God's understanding of a perfect world, **whether he created it or not**.

For the sake of the rest of this article I will speak as though Eden existed in space-time history instead of merely in the mind of God revealed to us through a narrative. This is just to make it simpler so I do not need to continuously clarify the two options. It's just a convention for simplicity sake, but it is one I happen to lean toward. If you do not, then just modify the language in your mind and run with it.

Eden

So, back to the original question; wasn't Eden free from any hint of difficulty, challenge, hardship or pain? Let's take a closer look at the Biblical data. In Genesis 3:16 Eve is told that God is going to "multiply" her pain at childbirth because of sin. The word for "multiply" that is used there

(Strong's word H7235) conveys the idea of "increase, enlarge, make great." Well one can only increase something that already exists! It is, interestingly, the same Hebrew word used when God instructed Adam and Eve to be fruitful and "multiply," a command that would have made no sense to issue before they existed. They must exist in order to multiply, and so must pain exist in order for God to multiply it. That punishment would have meant nothing to Eve unless she already understood what pain was. In other words, in some form or another giving birth was already an unpleasant experience. It would have been far less unpleasant at that time than it is these days, but we are still led to believe that it wasn't the kind of experience that Eve would have looked forward to.

Adam and Eve were also told that they could eat from pretty much any tree in the Garden.[19] But wait a minute! That means they needed to eat. If they needed to eat then we should naturally ask what would have happened if they didn't eat? Would they have felt hungry? Could they have starved to death? If nothing else it seems reasonable to expect that they would have experienced some kind of unpleasantness if they waited too long between meals; that discomfort would motivate them to eat. It seems rather pointless to provide food if there is no need for food.

But if there were two forms of unpleasantness (birth and hunger) why should we conclude they were the only forms of unpleasantness? That would seem pretty odd. It seems far more likely that various forms of unpleasantness existed, though they would have been a far cry from the anguishing pain that is possible these days.

Furthermore, God did not create them, plop them in a Garden and introduce them to the game of shuffleboard. And card games. And the Wii. On the contrary, he put them to work. They were told, in Genesis 1:28–30, to subdue the earth and that God had provided food for them. Again, though, they had to work for their food. Notice how the food did not float effortlessly from Heaven; they had to harvest trees and other plants. That required work which they were expected to do for themselves. God would provide sun and rain; they did the rest.

Indeed, the entire paradigm of creation is that God worked – which makes the Sabbath Rest (a major theme in the Old Testament) meaningful – and we are to imitate him. Work is not a result of the Fall, but is an example that God set and expected us to mimic even within the Garden of Eden.

So Eden had pain, it had hunger and it required work to keep it running. We do not have a very detailed picture of Eden – just enough for the

---

[19] Genesis 2:16.

theological purposes that God had in mind – but even these snapshots paint a picture of Eden that is a far cry from the "effortless pleasure" concept of a perfect world that many people these days seem to carry around with them. Even in the Garden of Eden character building opportunities abounded, though hardly to the same degree that we have them today.

What else is important, though, is that Eden had within it the potential to unfold into the world we see today. Indeed, God seemed to set up the circumstances in such a way that our present reality was an unavoidable product of one key ingredient that he introduced into the human spirit; free agency. He gave us the ability to make morally free choices. He did not create sin, but he made a world where sin was possible; the question was whether we would use our freedom to create it. As I described previously, free agency is the only logically possible way for his creatures to fulfill the potential he endowed them with. We could create vice, yes, but we could also create virtue.

The Fall

But surely he should have known it would go poorly. Surely he would have known we would sin. In fact I think he planned for it from the beginning. To follow the logic, I think that if Adam and Eve had not eaten the forbidden fruit, their obedience would have surprised God and ruined his entire plan! Consider this, what happened when they sinned? They were kicked out of the Garden.[20]

But wait! That means that the rest of the world was already more or less like our present world. Eden was not a description of the state of affairs in the entire cosmos, merely the state of affairs in one relatively tiny, insulated, pocket of real estate on Earth. Everything else in the universe, it would seem, looked quite different; like what we see today. The consequence of sin was not that the Garden of Eden fell into shambles, but rather that humanity was kicked out of their little bubble and forced to deal with the "real world." Eden remained perfect, humanity was simply evicted.

The point being that God already had the "real world" in place, waiting for them. Sin was inevitable, therefore God created Eden as a temporary holding place until humanity degraded exactly as he foresaw they would; a reality that he not only anticipated, but made specific provisions for right from the very first "Let there be…"

In fact, it could be argued, this present reality was what God really had in mind from the beginning, and Eden was just a temporary phase that

---

[20] Genesis 3:23–24.

humanity needed to pass through. And pass through it we would. He knew it would not last; he never intended it to! Why else would he create the rest of the world outside the Garden?

Of course that raises a whole series of subsequent theological questions about why God would bother with Eden at all; questions that are well worth considering, but none of which really have a lot of bearing on this discussion.

The New Earth

We are given hints in the Bible that the afterlife will be broadly modelled on what the Garden of Eden looked like. But before going any further, we ought to clarify that humanity will occupy the "New Earth" which is distinct from "Heaven" (Revelation 21:1). The reason this is somewhat important (rather than splitting theological hairs) is because we sometimes conceive of God's ultimate destination for us as being something fundamentally different from the present Earth. It will be very different in one sense, but remarkably similar in another. It will still be "Earth" in some broadly similar form, much like Eden was broadly similar to our present reality (trees, animals, work, and so on). We will not float around on clouds strumming on our harps, for instance; we will walk on streets, eat from trees and the nations will go about their business.[21]

Because the New Earth will be similar to the Garden of Eden we should not be surprised to learn that it will contain at least some challenges and probably some minor discomforts (at least relative to anything this world throws at us). Just as we were expected to work in the Garden of Eden the book of Revelation (21:24–26) describes a world within which there will still be nations going about their business and generating "riches" (or "glory and honour" – Strong's words G1391 and G5092). Of course the book of Revelation is highly metaphorical so we should be careful not to draw too many detailed conclusions (i.e. capitalism vs communism vs some other economic system) but it seems clear that it intends to convey the idea that there will be broad similarities between the basic framework of this world and the next. There was work in Eden and there will be work in the New Earth.

What about pain? If pain existed in Eden we should expect something

---

[21] A fascinating interview on this subject with N.T. Wright, renowned Christian theologian, author and retired bishop, can be read here: David Van Biema, *Time* magazine interview with Tom Wright, Feb. 7, 2008, "Christians Wrong About Heaven, Says Bishop," http://content.time.com/time/world/article/0,8599,1710844,00.html (accessed April 2016).

similar in the New Earth. Indeed much of what makes life in this earth rich and significant involves a good challenge and even a little pain at times. Conquering a mountain. Sailing around the world. Aerobatics in an airplane (a dream of mine!). C. S. Lewis in *The Problem of Pain* in the chapter on Hell explores the idea that there may be "pleasure" in Hell and even "pain" in Heaven – I put those words in quotations to remind us that they will be vastly different from our present understanding of the words – and he considers what those realities might mean.

In other words, if you were hoping to float gently in the clouds for all eternity, strumming a harp with not a care in the world, then the New Earth will be something of a disappointment for you. However, if you have developed any real character during your life on this earth you will realize the inherent beauty of a fruitful and applied life. The New Earth will introduce unimaginable glories that were never possible in this lifetime as we labour with the Creator himself!

The careful reader will notice that Revelation 21:4 very specifically says there will be no more pain in the New Earth. The Greek word used there (Strong's G4192) means something more like "anguish" then anything resembling "minor discomfort." It's like the difference between a gently stubbed toe and having one's toes forcibly removed with a rusty pair of pliers. God assures us there will be a total lack of the latter, but I see no reason to doubt the existence of the former in the New Earth.

Nobility in the New Earth

The book of Revelation makes it clear that there is a break between the old way of things and the new way of things (Revelation 21:1–4) but how far does that separation go? Does that mean we will have no recollection of our lives on Earth? Will we wake up one day and have no clue of who we are, where we are or how we got there? A major part of the entire process of hero-building is that our heroic nature is something which grows with time and experience (as I discussed at some length previously). If the former time and experience is completely stripped from our memory (and, consequently, our nature) then so is the entire hero-building process. We are back to square one – innocent as infants – which would make this entire earthly experience rather pointless.

While the New Earth will certainly entail a new order of things, it will not represent a full existential departure from the Old Earth. In 1 Corinthians 15:35–44 the apostle Paul illustrates how our resurrected bodies will be to our present bodies as a plant is to a seed. Distinct in one sense, but the new arises from the old; it both includes it and fulfills it. I suspect the New Earth will be much the same; a fulfillment of this Earth rather than scrapping the whole thing and starting from scratch with a completely different form of reality. In the New Earth we will be the same people we grew to become in this life, only we will have become purified and perfected from our corruption. But our heroism will survive death perfectly intact. After all, God only wants to get rid of the bad, not the good.

But could the differences between this Earth and the New Earth prove problematic? No more evil. No more suffering. This raises so many questions. First, how is this possible; are we not prone to sin? Even if God makes the New Earth perfect won't we mess it up again like we did in Eden? Second, how is nobility itself possible in a world without challenges (wasn't that the entire premise of my argument…)? Let's look at the second question first.

As I already mentioned, the New Earth will, in a manner of speaking, grow out of the soil of this Earth. The evil and suffering of this Earth will be part of the story of the New Earth. It will make up part of the furniture in the room, so to speak. There will be no new instances of either, but the many examples of evil and suffering that we have endured in this life will have become part of our story, our character. If I board a train in Edmonton, Alberta, and ride it all the way to Miami, Florida, it will always be the case that we passed through Edmonton on our journey, no matter where else our journey leads us or how long the journey is. If I remain on that train for all eternity then for all eternity my journey started in Edmonton. Because there is a connection between this world and the next the New Earth will always, by definition, "include" evil and suffering; those instances from this Earth. Nobility remains possible in the New Earth because of the suffering of this Earth.

As a simple illustration of this, when Jesus was resurrected he still bore the marks of his suffering.

A war veteran remains a hero many years after he has put down his rifle. If he never stands on the front lines again, his retirement in no way detracts from his heroic character and he continues to be honoured for his service as long as he lives. He has proven himself and he has earned his rest. The New Earth merely takes that concept of "rest" to a whole new level. We remain the heroes we became on this Earth as we engage in the delightful work of the New Earth; a form of permanent semi-retirement. And during that time we remain eternal heroes because of our choices on Earth. The war veteran who protected his nation's borders will be honoured for all eternity.

Can the New Earth remain perfect?

I said something previously that I wonder if you noticed. I wrote, "God created Eden knowing full well that the perfect world could not possibly remain in that state." That should lead the astute reader to ask how the perfect world could possibly remain perfect the second time around when it obviously failed the first time around.

While there will be substantial overlap between Eden and the New Earth, one significant difference separates the two: this Earth. What we will have in the New Earth that humanity completely lacked in Eden is life experience having passed through a world steeped in evil and suffering. Life experience under such circumstances produces character, and the combination of previously built character and continuously being in the presence of God makes it possible for morally free agents to retain their freedom while simultaneously maintaining their moral purity. God will make us pure of past sins through Jesus' sacrifice, and God will work with our developed nobility to ensure that we remain pure into the future.

It has been said (and I wish I could remember the source) that the older one gets the easier it becomes to resist temptation. What would have immediately trapped a young man or woman is a petty and easily resisted temptation for the elderly because our life experience helps us better understand the ridiculousness of succumbing to temptation, even if it remains tempting. As our lives extend into eternity the ability to resist temptation ought to become that much easier. Innocence is prone to failure, but experience more readily stands firm.

As I have pondered all this, one startling realization emerged. The New Earth that God actually designed humanity for is only theoretically possible if humanity passes through something like this Earth. While some people may think of this Earth as an unfortunate breakdown of the bus on the road to future glories, I have come to think of this Earth as some combination of a training ground, like a boot camp, and the refiner's fire. On the one hand this Earth is a necessary environment for character formation, and to give humanity a legitimate, relatively unimpeded, opportunity to become who they will be (whether good or evil). It is also a necessary refiner's fire; adversity often being the means of whittling away laziness, a lack of empathy for others and a wide range of other character flaws.

Naturally I am not proposing that admission into the New Earth is a product of human effort (I have read the Bible, after all) and God plays the necessary role in making it possible for us to ever be in his presence. While God alone makes it possible for us to enter his presence, our response to life's hardship plays a substantial role in forming the character of the person who ends up entering God's presence.

Objection 5 – Heroism Isn't Worth It

Suppose somebody might agree that human flourishing (i.e. the emergence of virtues such as heroism) is only possible in a world that looks something like this. It could be objected that heroism just isn't worth it. As nice as virtues may be, the price is just too high. What do we make of that?

What price is too high?

In the introductory overview for these objections I mentioned the interesting position God's critic is in when they claim that God is morally at fault for making this world. I will reiterate it here, briefly. In order to say that God did something wrong there is a long list of underlying assumptions behind that claim. First, the person making the claim knows the moral code at least as well as God, or possibly better. This is the only way that the person could claim that God made a moral error. Second, the person making the claim has all the relevant data in order to judge such a moral claim. And I do mean **all** the relevant data. The person needs to know everything good and bad that has ever happened throughout all of space-time history, as well as knowing all the causal effects between all the good and the bad, as well as everything that will one day happen as a direct or indirect result of all the good and bad that we see in this world. Just to be clear, that knowledge would also have to include the afterlife.

Most people are not going to hang their hat on the claim that they **know** God made a mistake, but rather that it **seems likely** that God made a mistake given what we know. It's a lousy world and God (we suppose) should have done better.

But that raises so many other questions. What, exactly, is the price?

What did we get for the price? How do we weigh the value of a full and rich life of, say, eighty years against the horror of fighting cancer for the last year or so? Are we going to claim that eighty years of human flourishing is outweighed by a single year of suffering? Some people say so. Some people claim that any single instance of suffering experienced by any single human throughout the entire history of the cosmos is enough to make this world morally repulsive. In other words that which is bad disproves God but that which is good does not prove him. Heads I win, tails you lose.

Others might accept a more balanced approach; some level of hardship and suffering may be permissible, but what humanity presently endures is well beyond that. And others, like myself, who see that hardship is the only means to character building, appreciate the bittersweet value of suffering and can understand, in broad strokes only, why God would allow his creation to endure what we endure. By analogy, a luxury car with a steep price tag will be met with various responses. Some people will agree that the price tag is appropriate to the car whether they can afford it or not. Others might say it is a little overpriced, or perhaps "it must be on sale." Still others, usually for principled reasons, might declare, "I wouldn't take that car if they gave it to me for free!" Agreeing on the value of a car is a simple task that humanity cannot reach consensus on; how much more difficult has it proven for us to agree on the value of heroism. There is one who knows the value of heroism better than we possibly could but it is his valuation we are presently questioning so his vote does not count.

This objection raises other questions. What constitutes bad and good? This may seem obvious on the face of it, but when you consider it more closely it is not always apparent. For instance, murdering somebody would be bad and saving somebody's life would be good – we can agree on that much – but what about the person who is neither murdered nor needs saving? When a person gets up in the morning, goes about their business that day relatively free from restriction and immanent life-threatening danger, then goes to bed at night in anticipation of a peaceful sleep, does that count as a good day? Nobody saved that person's life, which would have been a good thing, but surely life itself (going about one's business) is itself a good thing, even if that life was not saved from injury or death. Or, is that just "normal life" and it is neither good nor bad? It seems to me that it should be defined as good precisely because it is that kind of life that we are trying to preserve when we say it is bad to kill and good to save. It has inherent value that is worth preserving to the best of our abilities. But if that is the case then it seems trivially obvious, on the face of it, that the world has vastly more good than bad because there are far more people who live relatively trouble-free lives on any given day than those in dire circumstances.

Countless other questions are raised and all deserve serious consideration before we could confidently claim that the price is too high; heroism just is not worth it. Furthermore, one would have to demonstrate that the objection is not merely "I wouldn't pay that price" because clearly there are a lot of things I would never pay for but somebody else would. I would never spend my money on a luxury car but a lot of other people would. On the flip side, I would like to one day spend my money on a small homebuilt airplane but most other people would never think to spend their money on that. "To each his own" hardly carries any real weight in this conversation because we are trying to make a judgment call that would apply to humanity as a whole. Rather, the objection needs to come in the form "the price is unfair." In other words, the price is not wrong "for me" but wrong "for everybody," including God. The objection must be of an objective nature, not a subjective nature. It must be a fact that this world is immoral, not merely an opinion.

This objection is packed full of so many questions that one cannot seriously address it without first having a long and detailed conversation with whoever is making the objection in order to understand the grounds of their objection. I cannot imagine any form that the objection might take that meets the criteria of objectivity that I outlined in the last paragraph, but there are a lot of creative people out there.

How much is lost?

There is another side to this that I do not think the critics have sufficiently reflected upon and that is the question of how the law of unintended consequences may apply here. Some people might think it's as simple as getting rid of all the bad stuff so we can enjoy the good stuff.

But what if a lot more was at stake than just that? Imagine a world, for instance, where no person could ever go hungry because we did not need to work for our food. Perhaps we survived without food. Perhaps food floated effortlessly from the heavens, equally distributed over the face of the planet. Perhaps we lived by photosynthesis or something like that; use your imagination. Sounds great, what's the catch? Well, if there is no need to eat then we have just eliminated the entire food industry. That may not sound catastrophic on the face of it (they could find other jobs, right?), but let's rewind the tape of history. The history of civilization tended to centre around food. The agricultural industry played a significant role in the advent of civilization. Per Wikipedia, "All civilizations have depended on agriculture for subsistence."[22] That does not merely mean that individual

---

[22] Text available under the Creative Commons License: https://en.wikipedia.org/wiki/Civilization (page last modified 14 April 2016).

people need to eat, but that civilization itself – the growth of human enterprise – emerges in connection with agricultural activity. There is a lengthy discussion under the section entitled "Characteristics" of exactly how foundational the role of food is, not only with respect to human survival, but the emergence and growth of civilizations.

Because of the need for food, animals were domesticated. No need for food means no need for domesticated animals. The domestication of animals was a second major step on the road to civilization and industry. Indeed, the initial advances in technology were often associated, either directly or indirectly, with the need for humans to feed themselves. As technology began to develop, and as we found new ways to feed ourselves, humanity created cities, we wrote languages, we developed nations and states, we eventually learned medicine, science, waged wars, cured diseases, predicted weather and sent a man to the moon. For better (curing diseases) or worse (waging wars) civilization would not exist without the need to eat.

It would be impossible to say for certain how history would have unfolded if we never had the need to feed ourselves, but the research I have done suggests that agriculture and the domestication of animals played an absolutely pivotal role in the emergence of anything resembling civilization. If we could make the simple change of getting rid of the need to feed ourselves we would certainly eliminate all the starving children in Africa, but it seems very plausible that we would also eliminate much of what we cherish about civilization. Is it worth the price of all the great advances in civilization to eliminate hunger? I can see some reasons to say "yes" and some reasons to say "no." There is something inherently valuable and excellent about science, art, philosophy, architecture, medicine, engineering (okay, I'm biased), literature and all the other great accomplishments of humanity that must be considered when hypothesizing ways of eliminating suffering. Getting rid of all that, it seems to me, is no minor side effect.

Here is another example, what if we eliminated war? This sounds like a perfect idea with no negative consequences, but let us once again consider what else we might lose as a result. Some of the greatest advances in technology have come about in times of war, or have been developed (initially) for military purposes even in times of peace. I'm a bit of an airplane enthusiast and it has always amazed me that at the beginning of World War Two many air forces in the world still had at least a few wooden biplanes in their fleets. By the end of the war we had developed the first jet fighters and guided missiles. Shortly after the war, which lasted only six years, an airplane broke the sound barrier for the first time. From rickety biplanes to supersonic travel in a short six years, spurred on by war. These advances in technology led to substantial benefits for the civilian population by way of jet powered airliners, advances in navigation technology and the like. Indeed, during the cold war countless major technological advances were made to military technology that eventually made their way down to civilian use, bettering our lives. Global Positioning Systems (GPS) were initially created and operated by the American military. GPS provides countless benefits to your average civilian for peaceful purposes such as guiding industrial machinery to helping you find your way in a new city through your smartphone. Indeed, GPS is used for many other life-enhancing purposes that you and I are probably not aware of.

Countless other examples of civilian benefits from war, or the threat of war, could be provided, especially extending much further back into the recesses of human history, but these should be sufficient to illustrate that the elimination of war would result in other losses that may not be immediately apparent. From my own humble opinion I think getting rid of war would be well worth the loss of any technological gains we have enjoyed as a result of war. My point was not to defend war, but to illustrate the much broader consequences of making these kinds of wholesale and far-reaching changes. In the case of war it would seem easily justifiable to eliminate it. For other horrors we face, eliminating it is not so easily justified when we consider the baby that would be thrown out with the bath water. Simply saying, "God should get rid of ___" should never be accepted as a good idea without sufficient consideration of what other unexpected losses we might experience.

Before we confidently declare that the "price is too high" for this or that negative feature of the reality we find ourselves in, we need to consider whether that negative feature we wish to get rid of makes other positive features that we enjoy even possible in the first place. This careful analysis is very difficult to find from God's critics.

Heroism isn't all that great, anyway

My deeper suspicion, though, is that many people just don't understand the value of heroism, virtue and the "good life" (not to be confused with the hedonistic life). Those who object to the state of this world, knowing that heroism would be lost in their "perfect world," must consider the absence of human flourishing to be an acceptable price to pay. Getting rid of all the heroes, including the hero within, is worth it. In fact, losing any opportunity for heroism is worth the price.

I suspect that people who wish this world lacked opportunities for heroism have either not yet been faced with the opportunity to develop their own heroic natures or they have not taken advantage of the opportunity when it was presented. If you have ever volunteered in a soup kitchen then you probably instinctively know the inherent value of serving others; service that would never be required in a world without hunger. If you have ever given large sums of money to somebody in need (or preferably a registered charity!) knowing that you could have spent it on a new flat screen TV then you probably instinctively know the inherent value of sacrificing your own comfort and entertainment for the betterment of others facing exceptional difficulty. If you have ever visited with an elderly person just so they have something to do during the day, when you could have used that time to get caught up on Facebook or watch cat videos on YouTube, then you probably know the inherent value of thinking of others before yourself.

Or, of course, the vocational heroes that I previously praised – soldiers, police, firemen, paramedics, doctors and many more – they probably generally have a very good understanding of the deep soul-level fulfillment that heroism entails. The cancer victim who stands tall and joyously lives the rest of their shortened life to the fullest is a picture of heroic beauty that could never be intellectually explained to those who do not instinctively grasp it. To prefer a world without any of that, just for the sake of avoiding suffering, is to reveal a little bit about the status of one's own heroic nature. Yes we should absolutely dream of, and fight for, a world with less suffering – indeed we would be psychotic not to long for that – but we also instinctively understand the magnificence of rising to the occasion, of facing the horror and tackling it. When we understand what would be lost – that we would all be reduced to couch-surfing blobs of pleasure-craving flesh – surely most of us can instinctively realize that there is something inherently better about our imperfect world filled with suffering heroes if that is the only logical alternative.

If you don't get that, I cannot explain it. Maybe try volunteering at a soup kitchen if you seriously want to understand. I am reminded of a quote from the book *Handbook of Christian Apologetics* as the authors describe an argument for the existence of God. (page 81)

The Argument from Aesthetic Experience

- There is the music of Johann Sebastian Bach.

- Therefore there must be a God.

You either see this one or you don't.

That's it. That's the end of their entire argument and its exploration and defense. A single sentence. When I first read it I was bothered by it. No logical exposition? No further analysis and deflection of criticism? At first that annoyed my analytical mind, but I came to understand that this is one of those issues in life that is a foundation of logic, not something arrived at via logic. Sometimes the truth of an idea is either grasped or it is not and when it is not then there is no further logical analysis that will make it any clearer.

The music of Johann Sebastian Bach is beautiful. You either get that or you do not. Heroism, similarly, is of great moral value. Striving for the peak of our human potential is the imperative of every soul on earth. The journey of conquest through the jungles of our own fears and frailties in order to emerge on the other side, bruised and battered, but still substantially better people, is a journey worth taking. Pain and suffering, for the most part, are prices worth paying to become the people we were intended to be. We may wrestle with philosophical implications of the extent and degree of what is horrible with our world, but the prospect of dismissing it altogether is the domain of those who wish to embrace a subhuman existence. It is a proposition put forth by those who yearn for the life of a sea sponge instead of the life of a knight in shining armour, slaying the dragon and saving the damsel from imminent danger. Or the tale of a valiant soldier on the front lines of battle against an evil empire, seizing his buddy's arm and gasping with his dying breath, "Tell my wife I love her!" You were made for greatness – a costly, painful greatness – you ought to rise to the occasion. Seize the day!

You either see this one or you don't.

Objection 6 – Animal Suffering

So what about the animals? What are we to make of their suffering? If the accepted history of the world is to be believed then they've been around a lot longer than we have, living and dying for millions of years before the first humans ever arrived. Surely all that animal suffering is impossible to reckon with from a theistic point of view. What a senseless horror!

The epistemic barrier

Some time ago the philosopher Thomas Nagel wrote an interesting essay in which he pondered what it might be like to be a bat.[23] It has been a fairly influential essay in philosophical circles precisely because it raises a question that not too many people often think about. Do we really know what it is like to experience life from any perspective other than our own? Even when it comes to other humans we are very limited. I cannot stand the smell of coffee but other people absolutely love it. I have no idea what it is like to experience the pleasure (so I'm told) of sipping a cup of coffee. And I have no idea what it would be like to be a soldier, though I am grateful for those who are. I cannot imagine being a doctor who delivers babies. I just don't

---

[23] It is not difficult to find a copy of the article on the internet if you care to read it (see below for one example), though it is not necessary for the remainder of my argument. To be clear, Nagel was not writing on the subject of animal suffering and I have no idea what his views were on the subject. I'm just using his acknowledgement of the epistemic barrier as a handy launching point for these observations.

Thomas Nagel, "What Is It Like to Be a Bat?" in *The Philosophical Review*, vol. 83, no. 4 (Oct. 1974), 435–450, published by Duke University Press, DOI: 10.2307/2183914, http://www.jstor.org/stable/2183914 (accessed April 2016).

like all that blood and stuff.

Between humans there is what we might call an "epistemic barrier" in that there are certain aspects of the experiences of other human beings that I do not have. Philosophers call these "first person" perspectives. Indeed, not only do I not have those experiences of others, I never could, even in theory. When another person sees the colour red, that is their experience of the colour red, not mine. In all likelihood our experiences are remarkably similar, of course, but in other cases the experiences will be quite different (sipping coffee, for instance).

So what about animals? Can I imagine what it might be like to be a bat as Nagel mused? Of course not. I could not even begin to conjure up an accurate image of how a bat experiences the world around them. I'm not always a fan of the dark but no bat would ever care about the lack of light. Flying? Only in an airplane.

But there must be some overlap, right? More to the point of the subject of this book, animals must experience pain and suffering. I went for a walk during a rainy day and I saw worms stretched out on the sidewalk. They were dying, or would be soon when the robins got them. Were they in pain? I'm not so sure they were. Frankly whatever tiny brain they have hardly seems up to the task of really processing pain. Were they terrified? Was there a sense of horror at their own impending demise similar to what we might experience? Is the movie *A Bug's Life* a documentary? I'm not convinced they understand enough about the world around them and their place in the world to really be terrified by anything.

Okay, so maybe we shouldn't worry about the really simple forms of life, but surely the higher forms of life have experiences similar to ours. Surely dogs, cats, horses, lions, elephants, dolphins and so many other forms of advanced life have broad overlap in their mental and emotional (even moral?) capacities as we do. If you've played with dogs and cats you will have noticed that there certainly seems to be a high level of understanding and interaction that they are capable of.[24]

It seems to me that this is the root of the issue; to what extent are the experiences of humans and advanced animals similar? Broadly speaking it seems we have two possibilities, either there is substantial similarly between humans and animals or there is not.

Suppose animals are like humans

First let us suppose there is broad overlap between humans and the higher

---

[24] Unless otherwise noted all subsequent references to animals are in reference to these "higher forms" of animals.

forms of animals. Let us suppose that animals feel pain. Not just pain, they feel horror at the possibility of their own demise (if it ever came to that). They feel empathy and even understand some simple form of right and wrong. In other words, let's assume animals are quite a bit like us, even if the overlap is not perfect. The basic ingredients are there but in a much simpler form.

If that is the case then it seems to me that whatever "problem of suffering" exists in humanity also exists (in a similar form) in animals. We have this problem that we have to deal with and, if animals are similar to us, then so do the animals. If there is a solution to the problem for humanity, it seems to me that there would probably be a relatively similar solution for animals. For instance, if suffering offers humans the possibility for heroism then animals probably have something similar going on, though at a simplified scale. We know the difference, for instance, between the heroism of a police dog and the barbarism of those ravage beasts that guard the junk yard.

If that is the case, though – if animals and humans have broadly overlapping emotional and moral realities – then do we really add anything to the conversation by bringing animals into the discussion? It seems that we do not. Animal suffering, then, falls into roughly the same category as human suffering and the philosophical discussion has gone nowhere by bringing up animal suffering. Whatever insights we glean from our own suffering are sufficient to inform the conversation; no animals needed.

Suppose animals are unlike humans

But what about the other option; what if the animal experience of the world is very dissimilar to our own? Indeed, as the article on animal suffering at Wikipedia points out, the question of animal suffering is an extremely wide open question with no obvious answer.

> However, for non-human animals, it is harder, if even possible, to know whether an emotional experience has occurred.

Animals without human language cannot report their feelings, and whether they are conscious and capable of suffering has been a matter of some debate. As described at Wikipedia, "…Although it is likely that some animals have at least simple conscious thoughts and feelings, some authors continue to question how reliably animal mental states can be determined."[25]

---

[25] Text available under the Creative Commons License: https://en.wikipedia.org/wiki/Pain_in_animals (page last modified 18 April 2016).

[*The Stanford Encyclopedia of Philosophy* dives in at a little more depth in its article on animal consciousness.[26] Even there the debate appears to be far from settled.]

Even though it appears as though animals are suffering when their bodies are damaged, the reality is that even the simplest forms of life (amoebas for instance, as Wikipedia points out) also appear to "writhe" if exposed to harmful chemicals. Surely amoebas are not emotionally tormented if they are harmed. If they are not, then higher life forms may also be devoid of suffering as we understand it. It is possible that even the highest non-human life form has an experience of pain that is wildly different from our own, if they experience pain at all. They might just have an awareness that something is wrong without ever actually "feeling" the pain as an emotional experience. When injured, their body simply reacts and their reaction looks, on the outside, like what we might do if we were in pain.

If their experience is so different from ours that we cannot understand it, once again I ask what value there is in discussing animal suffering vis-à-vis human suffering. Indeed, they may not even suffer at all in the sense that we are familiar with and if they do, what do we really know, beyond a shadow of a doubt, about their experience of suffering? In this case animal suffering adds nothing to the conversation because we have absolutely no hard data to work with. Zilch. Only speculation and assumptions. Until some human can answer the question of "what is it like to be a bat?" the question of animal suffering does not really add any clarity to the picture that human suffering does not already provide.

Until we do know, any conclusion we may draw from animal suffering, it turns out, is nothing but a "suffering of the gaps" argument. We can get mad at God for animal suffering only if we draw conclusions about animal suffering that go far beyond all the available data. Arguments based on animal suffering are arguments from ignorance. That is not a very responsible form of persuasion. We should deal with what we know rather than speculating about what we may never, even in theory, be able to know.

Blindsight

There is a certain phenomenon in humanity that may shed some light on this subject; it is called blindsight. A person with this ailment is partially blind, at least in part of their field of vision. If you place a glass of water on

---

[26] Colin Allen and Michael Trestman, "Animal Consciousness," *The Stanford Encyclopedia of Philosophy* (Summer 2015), Edward N. Zalta (ed.), http://plato.stanford.edu/entries/consciousness-animal/#currsci-pain (accessed April 2016).

the table in front of them they would not be aware of it. You might ask them what is on the table in front of them and they would say that they have no idea. You might suggest that they reach out and grab the cup, they would naturally resist; "what cup?" If you were to push the issue, and if they were to agree to "try" they would (often, not always) reach out and successfully grab it.

What's going on here? How can they fail to see the glass of water, yet reach out and grab it when they decide to give it a shot? The nature of the ailment is fascinating because the light signals from the glass of water are being received by their eyes and transmitted to their brain, and even **processed by their brain**, but that information is not passed along to their consciousness. In other words, their **brain** is well aware of the glass of water, but their **mind** is not. When they push themselves to reach for something their mind is unaware of, their brain figures out what's going on and does what it needs to do. It controls the rest of the body and causes it to do what is necessary in order to accomplish its goal. All of that occurs without any conscious awareness of the glass of water.

This illustrates the possibility that actions of the body may be controlled by the brain without consciousness getting involved. The brain is obviously quite active in the whole process, but the mind is being kept out of the loop. The person has no experience of the external stimuli. What is critical in all this, however, is the fact that the actions of the body controlled only by the brain (no conscious input) appear virtually identical to what the actions of the body would have been if the person's mind were in charge. From the outside we would not know whether it was a conscious mind reaching for the glass, or an impulsive brain reaching for the glass.

Consider the implications of this with respect to our conversation about animal suffering. If it is possible for a human brain to "respond appropriately" to external stimuli without the need for conscious awareness, then it certainly seems plausible that animal brains may be able to respond appropriately to external stimuli without the need for conscious awareness. In other words it is possible that animals do not experience the world in the same way that we do, but their brains control their functions in a manner similar to humans with blindsight. With respect to pain, this could easily mean that the nerve endings throughout their body are sending signals to their brain which are being interpreted by the brain, appropriate response actions are determined by the brain and reaction signals are sent back to the appropriate body parts, all without any conscious experience of pain. If the animal steps on something sharp, it pulls back its leg but it might do that in the absence of any experience of pain. It may be the case that the animal brain processes the inputs but the animal's mind (if it has one) experiences nothing, in the same way that the brain of a person with blindsight processes the sensory data while the person themselves experiences nothing of what the brain is dealing with.

A personal example

In fact, I can supply a similar example from my own experience. I was framing houses one summer and I accidentally shot myself in the thumb with a nail gun. You can still see the scar today if we ever meet in person (left thumb, just below the knuckle). What I describe next all happened within a fraction of a second. The nail gun went off twice (this happens sometimes with amateurs like me) and the first nail shot into the piece of lumber, the recoil caused the nail gun to "bounce" to the edge of the lumber, and the second nail missed the lumber. It flew through the air and impacted my thumb. My first brief impression (I hadn't enough time to formulate a full thought yet) was a sense of general concern because it's always dangerous when the nail gun fires twice. My second brief impression (again, too soon for a thought) was curiosity about why my left arm was flailing about. At this point I (as in my conscious self) took back control of my body, moved my left arm so my eyes could see, and there was a nail, lodged in my left thumb. Now that I knew (as in, my mind knew, not just my brain) what the problem was, I consciously shook my left arm around all the more vigorously to dislodge the nail, which worked.

Of course, if calmer heads had prevailed I would have known that flinging the nail out probably wasn't the best idea, but this all happened before the calmer head wandered on to the scene.

Interestingly, it didn't hurt. Not before and not after it came out; it lodged in the bone without hitting any muscle. Even without pain, though, my brain knew something had gone wrong, knew it had to do with my left thumb, and knew what to do about it. My brain knew all of this before "I" did. My mind was playing catch-up the entire time. And the appropriate course of action my brain came up with was similar to what my mind resolved to do once it was brought up to speed on the situation.

Again, none of this is intended to prove that animals do not experience pain, but to simply remind us that agnosticism on the subject is the best conclusion given the available evidence and the possibility that their brains are causing their bodies to respond to pain without any conscious experience of pain. In this case there is not enough data to reasonably extrapolate from human experiences to animal experiences with any real confidence.

Possible or plausible?

But we should ask ourselves whether the mere fact that it is possible that animals merely appear conscious makes that a truly plausible option? After all, just about any strange explanation of reality is "possible." It is possible, one could argue, that we are all brains in vats instead of really alive in the world. Possibility alone counts for very little unless we have reason to take these "possibilities" seriously. I have little reason to take seriously the idea that I am really just a brain in a vat. So the question needs asking, even if we cannot prove whether animals do or do not experience pain (as opposed to merely responding to dangerous stimuli) do we have any good reason to think animals are all that different from us? They have brains and we have brains. Some of their brains are really quite similar to ours. If the structure is similar and the reactions are similar (from the perspective of the third-person observer) it seems reasonable to conclude the experiences are similar.

First quick comment, the same thing could be said of blindsight. The brain structure is similar and the response (reaching for the glass) is similar. However, even with these similarities we would obviously be wrong if we drew the conclusion that the experiences are the same. What blindsight should teach us is that similarity in external behaviour is not proof of similarity in conscious experience.

But more to the point, do we have reason to believe that humans are in some sense uniquely separate from other animals? I would suggest we do have reason to think that humans are unique. In fact, I would suggest we have multiple reasons to suspect (though, again, not enough evidence to conclude anything with certainty) that the line of consciousness may be at the level of humans and not below. For starters, humans create zoos to showcase animals, but no animal has ever created a zoo to showcase humans. Furthermore, we have multiple languages with hundreds of thousands of words, whereas the smartest animals can be taught a bit of sign language and that's it (the scientists who conducted the study ended up doubting that animals could ever "form sentences and express ideas"[27]). We have built the Hoover dam to generate electricity; beavers just need a place to swim. We have flown faster than the speed of sound and landed a man on the moon; no ground-based animal has ever created a flying machine. We have the Sistine Chapel, Handel's Messiah, the works of Shakespeare and Aristotle, the Pyramids, the Great Wall of China, the Hubble telescope, the Hadron collider and so much more.

Intelligence in the animal kingdom seems to roughly increase with the size of the animal's brain, but that last step from any other animal up to humans is, frankly, a really big step. Something is going on in our

---

[27] For more info, cf. "The Chimp That Learned Sign Language," May 28, 2008, http://www.npr.org/2008/05/28/90516132/the-chimp-that-learned-sign-language (accessed April 2016).

consciousness that sets us apart from anything else in the animal kingdom. And the margin is anything but slim. The difference has been history-changing.

Intelligence, of course, is not necessarily connected to the experience of pain, and I am not claiming it is. All I am saying is that we can see that something fairly significant goes on in the minds of humans that is not found, except in trace quantities, in the rest of the animal kingdom. If these kinds of substantial differences exist in one area of our being it is not unreasonable to speculate that other differences may also exist, and the conscious experience of external stimuli (including pain) may certainly be quite different.

So, again, we have no solid data to conclude either way with respect to animal pain, but we have several lines of reasoning that lead us to conclude that

- The data is too fuzzy to draw any solid conclusions, and
- It is certainly plausible that the animal experience of reality is fundamentally different from the human experience of reality, including pain.

The only reasonable conclusion is agnosticism (though one may lean this way or that). However, given the absence of irrefutable evidence either way about animal pain and suffering, drawing solid metaphysical conclusions is presumptuous at best. The entire discussion of the possibility of animal suffering is a pointless red herring founded on speculation and theories, never on hard data. Let's stick to what we know rather than trying to draw conclusions from what we do not know.

Conclusion

So if animal suffering is like human suffering then the solution to the problem of suffering for animals will be similar to the solution to the problem for humans (if there is a solution). No value is added in discussing animal suffering. If animal "suffering" is unlike human suffering – and we have reasons to believe this is a plausible (though unproven) scenario – then we have no grounds on which to draw any firm conclusions of any kind. No value is added in discussing animal suffering. Either way animal suffering, it turns out, is a red herring. We will not learn anything new from animal suffering that we would not have learned from human suffering. We might as well just focus on that subject about which we have a fairly high degree of certainty instead of idly speculating on a subject that we may, in fact, be wildly wrong about anyway.

Now, don't go drawing a whole bunch of unwarranted conclusions based on what I've just said. I don't flog cats or anything. As humans I believe we have a duty to preserve life on this planet to the best of our ability and if our duty to manage the planet requires us to end animal life (or if we just want to eat) then we should treat animals as though they are fully capable of experiencing the same feelings we have. In other words, given our state of relative uncertainty we ought to err on the side of ethical caution. However, assuming they have experiences like ours, for the sake of erring on the side of caution, does not mean we should assume they have experiences like ours in order to draw philosophical conclusions. Eco-responsibility looks vastly different from philosophical responsibility.

God, on the other hand, is not ignorant of animal experiences and will have dealt with the situation appropriately. Any attempt on our part to draw firm conclusions about God's character based on what we see in the animal kingdom is speculation, as wild as many of the animals we are discussing.

Afterthoughts

When I originally wrote the blog articles that comprised the previous chapters I wondered if I would still hold to the same conclusions after the initial shock and pain of the experience had subsided. It's been three years now and I still stand behind what I've written, which is why I have been motivated to put it into book form.

However, I had some follow-up reflections in the years since catastrophe struck.

Further benefits of suffering

I outlined a number of benefits of enduring suffering, benefits that would be impossible in the absence of suffering. But there was an additional benefit I did not really notice until much later, after the situation had passed. As I alluded to in the dedication to this book, I know I'm not the easiest guy to be married to. I have a very unusual personality type, as is evidenced by the fact that I wrote an analytical response to suffering. Who does that? When we suffer, a careful analysis of the situation is usually the furthest thing from our minds, right? Well, not my mind, I guess. Besides that obviously anomalous character trait, I have a long list of other quirks as well. And, just to be fair, Denise has her own difficulties that she will admit to, so we both brought some personal challenges to our marriage.

And our marriage wasn't anywhere close to the fairy tale that many people believe marriage is supposed to be. We were nowhere close to separating, but things had certainly been rather rocky in the years prior to the event. Voices had been raised on numerous occasions. I'll leave it at that.

Since her time in the hospital, though, things changed. It didn't happen right away – which is part of the reason I didn't blog about this side effect at the time – but change did gradually take place. The difficulties we were going through gradually didn't seem so significant. Our differences became increasingly trivial. There are times I still get frustrated with her (and she gets upset with me quite frequently, too), but when I'm mad at her I sometimes find my mind wandering back to the moment I first saw her in ER. At that moment, in that ER room, I no longer had a wife. She was gone. Her body was still moving – technically "functioning" by some loose definition of the word – but there was no evidence of mental activity behind her eyes. Even if her heart kept pumping and her physical body somehow made it through the next few days, I was fully convinced that her self, her mind, her soul had already moved on.

When an image like that haunts you for the rest of your life, everything else in your little corner of the world gets shuffled. That event has caused me to reconsider a lot of things in life, and a significant amount of that reflection centred on my marriage. As a result, I am far more patient when she pushes my buttons and I am far more careful not to push hers. We still don't have as many date nights as we'd like (the kids aren't quite old enough to stay home alone yet), but they are becoming more frequent. No, we have not arrived at "happily ever after" – which is a fictitious goal anyway – but the improvements have been palpable.

I've had a chance to do some public speaking at churches in the wake of this whole episode. I give a few illustrations when I describe how something like this can serve to solidify relationships. For instance, imagine a mother whose son has gone off to war receiving the dreaded letter in the mail: "We regret to inform you…"

Then imagine, one day, that her son walks up to the door. The letter had been written in error. She would hug her son more tightly on that day than on any day prior and probably any day after. Her joy (confused joy, admittedly) would be unimaginable. I wrote a chapter describing how our default perspective will influence our interpretation of the problem of pain, as we are going through it, but I failed to consider how enduring a painful process can then provide us with a new perspective on life. A married man may love his wife, but something about that love fundamentally changes when he almost loses her. For me, that love grew deeper, richer, more sombre and more unshakeable. It's a kind of love that was unimaginable to me before Denise was almost lost to me.

Pain, in a culture of comfort

Speaking of perspective, another interesting observation about suffering has been made (not only by me). It seems those who suffer least, particularly those who live in Western comfort, seem most bothered by suffering. An interesting reality about God's critics is that they are predominantly found in places like Europe and North America where we have, unquestionably, the highest living standard anywhere in the world, and any time in human history. Why is that? Why are people who do not suffer liable to shake their fist at God, whereas those who do suffer are more liable to reach their open hand out to God?

I have a theory. Can you tell me the last time you have tossed and turned at night because you did not win a gold medal at the last Olympic games? Personally, I've never lost any sleep for that reason, though I've lost sleep for other reasons. It has never bothered me, even once, that I haven't won a gold medal at any Olympic games. It's probably never bothered you.

But I'll bet it really bugs the guy who won the silver medal. I'll bet he has tossed and turned. I'll bet he has pounded his fist on the table. So close, yet still so far away.

Of all the humans on earth, the silver medalist can demonstrate that he is the second best on the face of the planet at his particular sport. In all likelihood I probably cannot even compete at all. In fact, that person could easily beat millions of people at their particular sport, so why might he be upset when he has something that the overwhelming majority of humans will never have?

There's something interesting about being closer to some goal that makes not meeting it all the more painful. This is a strange aspect of human psychology. The woman who loses a child to disease in some small village in Africa where many children regularly die of disease will mourn, of course, but she may not be as devastated as a woman in Toronto who loses a child to the same disease. In Toronto the expectation, the normal course of events, is that babies survive. The further we are from some utopian version of reality the less bothered we become that it is so far away. The closer we approach it, the more frustrating the remaining gap becomes.

And so, ironically, I am convinced that one unintended consequence of all our medical advances, all our technological improvements, all our safety initiatives is that they have made us hypersensitive to any suffering that comes our way. Such experiences are far more likely to shake us to our very core and force us into some existential crisis. Having little or no prior experience with suffering, we simply don't know how to handle it.

Indeed, the fact that my life was so utterly jarred by the events described is further testimony to the relative comfort I have lived in. I can almost hear somebody from a war-torn, starvation-ravaged country listening to Denise's story and protesting, "That's your biggest problem?!" She spent a mere five weeks in the hospital with absolutely zero residual effects and that inspired a book on suffering. Compared to folks in those situations, what do I really know about suffering?

It is so easy, isn't it, to shake our fists at God when some relatively minor tragedy strikes – even something less significant than what Denise went through – while simultaneously forgetting to lift our hands in gratitude at the fact that this relatively minor tragedy is the most catastrophic struggle we've had to endure. I might get angry with God because my wife almost died, but how often to I remember to thank him that she lives?

I still have a lot of character growth to go, it would seem. So do many of us in advanced - comfortable - nations.

Suffering sucks

A wise man once, maybe twice, pointed out to me that even if suffering could be fully explained – if every instance and magnitude of suffering could be completely explained and justified to everybody's satisfaction – suffering is still suffering.

In the introduction to this book I clarified that my intent was not to bring comfort. But when a person is suffering it is comfort, not answers, that is usually their primary need. For me, personally, I found that many of these reflections did bring an element of comfort, so answers absolutely have their place. But at a time like that a person needs a shoulder to cry on more than they need an answer to ponder. Ideally we can provide both, but let us not forget to offer the open arms before we offer the open mouth.

God's answer to suffering – the cross

In the first chapter I described why Jesus was the only one worth talking to during a time like this because he is the only person in history with a track record of reliably producing the kind of results we were hoping for. But there is another key reason to lean on Jesus during such times.

As I have hopefully explained, the world in its present state may very well be the ideal world in which moral freedom is meaningfully maintained, and in which the opportunity for heroism is most effectively extended to humanity. How could God "improve" on this world without sacrificing one of those two features? But even if the end result of this world is both magnificent and justifiable, the process still sucks (see above).

However, God didn't just sit back in the comfort of Heaven, look down on us in pity, and think to himself, "Oh, boy, I can't wait till this part is over!" On the contrary, he condescended to our level. He became one of us in the person of Jesus. God stepped foot on this earth in part as an act of solidarity. To suffer with us. He offered both the open arms and the open mouth.

And his life on earth was not one of "creature comforts." Born in a barn, his first crib was a feeding trough for animals. During his ministry he was constantly harassed by the religious leaders. Eventually it cost him his life, but not in some quick and painless fashion. The physical suffering he endured during his execution vastly surpasses anything most of us could even fathom, hence the word "excruciating" – from the Latin words *ex cruciatus*: out of the cross. Can God understand our suffering? The more pressing question is whether we could possibly understand God's suffering!

He did not merely endure suffering, he endured evil. Being God, Jesus is, by definition, the only morally perfect man to walk this earth. Despite his moral perfection he was put through a sham trial, mocked, beaten and hung naked as passersby spat on him. The Creator, shunned by his own creation.

And this is what I find to be the most beautiful theology from any of the world religions. Atheism claims there is no God; when it comes to suffering we are on our own. Furthermore, there cannot be any ultimate purpose to suffering along the lines of preparing our character for the next life because when we die it's all over. Islam says nothing of God becoming human. In the conversations I've had with Muslims they make it clear that Islam would consider the very idea preposterous. God is "out there" and we are "down here" and God will never traverse that gap.

In Christianity, however, God walked with us in the Garden of Eden, until we disobeyed him. He walked with us, even carrying his own cross, until we executed him. And he will walk with us again throughout eternity in the New Earth, after he forgives us.

> Therefore, since the children have flesh and blood, he himself also shared the same things, so that by his death he might destroy the one who has the power of death … Because he himself suffered when he was tempted, he is able to help those who are being tempted.
>
> (Hebrews 2:14, 18 ISV)

Section 2

Thought experiment

Perfect World – Introduction

I was so intrigued by the concept of a world devoid of suffering (as discussed in a previous chapter) that I wrote a short story to examine what such a world would plausibly look like. What such a world would actually look like is obviously an unknown, but what follows is my best guess. I have done my best to represent what I believe would be the most likely outcome. Though it is clearly quite over the top in many respects, I do believe each consequence follows naturally and unavoidably from the form of perfection that the subject of the story demands.

Perfect World – The Offer

It's a long story how I arrived at the café so I'll just give you the short version. I died. The afterlife was not what I expected – in part because, honestly, I wasn't expecting any afterlife. However, even in my wildest dreams I never would have imagined – even the religious literature I had read said nothing like this – that I would end up in a coffee shop with God. I ordered my usual and God ordered... well, I don't remember. It might have just been a simple tea. Having coffee with God was rather unexpected, so some of the details of the experience are a little fuzzy.

He covered the costs. He's nicer than I expected. I wasn't sure what to make of all that Old Testament stuff of warmongering and killing people who look at him the wrong way.

The rest of the coffee shop was abuzz with people sipping their lattes, teas, coffees and other beverages. I wasn't clear whether this was part of Heaven or some place on Earth. There was a young mom ordering a drink while trying to keep her fussy child at bay. A young couple sat two tables over, gazing in each other's eyes, giggling and nervous. An elderly man, still full of vitality and young in his demeanour, sat at the very next table, seemingly oblivious to the fact that he was within arm's reach of his Creator.

And why would he? God seemed to just fit in like any other human. Not particularly tall. No striking features. It occurred to me upon further reflection that I could not remember any specific detail about his appearance at all. He might have had a moustache. Was his hair curly? He seemed just as real as the elderly man sitting next to us, though I'm sure I could have remembered more details about the man (trimmed goatee, slightly outdated fashion sense, grey hair; almost professorial) than about God who was sitting across from me, slowly turning his cup as though he were deep in thought.

"So, let's get the awkward stuff out of the way. You didn't think I existed," he finally said.

Well, how does one respond to that? Lying didn't seem like it would serve any purpose at all.

"No, I did not," I answered. Somehow I didn't fear him and his wrath. He bought me an iced capp, after all. It didn't seem as though he were here to settle any scores.

"That always bothered me. But I guess we cleared up that little misunderstanding," he said with a slight smile. It wasn't a derogatory smirk that seemed to say, "Hah, I proved you wrong," but rather the kind that could not be avoided, given the irony of the situation.

"Well, you know, it's pretty hard to believe in you with all that's wrong with the world."

He looked past me, out the window. His gaze tracked somebody outside the coffee shop making their way to the entrance. A slight turn of my head and I could see who he was watching. With some fumbling of the door a young man with crutches finally made his way in. The young mom with the fussy kids held the door for him; she was on her way out. Fairly athletic, though somewhat unkempt, he looked to be in his twenties. His crutches gave him the support he needed as he hobbled into the café, the lower part of one leg missing from the knee down.

"Like him," I said. "Living in a world where people could lose their limbs is pretty awful."

"It was very awful for him," God answered.

He agreed with me?

"You think the world should have been different," he ventured.

"Many people do. In fact, even those who believe in you... er..." I had to change my language now, the circumstances were obviously quite different than during my life, "I mean, even those who knew about you struggled a lot with how they were supposed to understand all the difficulties of life. You know, given your omnipotence, omniscience, 'God of love' and all that."

"Oh, yes, I was very aware of that. The book of Job was supposed to..." He paused. It seemed he trailed into his own thoughts momentarily.

"I wonder, would you have done it differently?" he asked.

I was about to answer, "Yes, of course," but I hesitated. I wasn't dealing with some halfwit Christian here who had never thought about these issues and instead relied on their weekly "fix" of emotional manipulation to sustain their pitiful faith. This was different. He was different. And yet, I'm not sure my answer would really be all that different. I made those claims not merely because I knew it grated on Christians but because I really believed they were true. Could I back down now?

"It seems possible to imagine some improvements that could be made, yes," I answered.

God turned his cup some more. Gently, with his fingertips.

"So you feel that you could improve this world. I see. I suspect you have some specific improvements in mind?" he asked.

He was being gracious. Any God worthy of the title knew full well what I had said throughout my life, what I had thought throughout my life and what I was thinking at that moment. Yet he politely condescended to the level of a normal person. I was almost starting to like him.

"We all have some improvements in mind," I finally conceded.

"Do you believe that I would have considered those as well?" he wondered.

I guess I hadn't really taken that possibility seriously because I didn't think he really existed anyway. I suppose if I had taken the possibility of his existence seriously then I might have realized that he knows a whole lot more than I do and I could never know his reasons. But because he was on par with Bigfoot in my mind I never really treated the suffering of humanity as anything more than a mind game I would play with ill-prepared Christians. It seemed obviously true; why bother with the details?

"I suppose you probably did," I responded, "but it seems unfathomable from our perspective that a world like this could be morally justifiable."

I looked back over to the athletic young man, the amputee.

"Did he have to lose his leg?" I asked, "What was the reason for that?"

"Do you think there could be a good reason? Is that even possible to believe?"

During my life I had never been open to the idea that there was a legitimate reason. Reasons, perhaps, but none of them could possibly be sufficient. The phrase "gratuitous suffering" rolled off my tongue like water over Niagara Falls. I just assumed there was no reason good enough. Now I was second-guessing.

Could there have been a good reason? Surely not! Could not the divine Creator of the universe have stepped in and prevented that tragedy without fundamentally altering the course of human history? There didn't seem to be much point in pretending to think other than I did.

"It is very difficult to believe that the majority of suffering could have a good reason," I replied. "Is there a good reason why thousands of children die every year due to starvation?"

God just kept turning his cup. Slowly. Methodically. I couldn't tell, but it seemed as though his eyes were tearing up.

"Do you think you could do better?" he asked again.

"I think I could." It sounded arrogant to say but the obviousness of what was wrong with the world seemed inescapable. Some of the smartest men in history on both sides of the theism-atheism debate have envisioned a better world. The ingredients seemed obvious. Yes, even though it sounded arrogant to say it to God himself, I figured I might as well be honest.

"Would you like to try?" he asked.

What? Did I hear that right?

I sat back. Stunned. Was he handing me control of the universe? Was this Heaven, Hell or just some dream? Had I really died? Perhaps I was just hallucinating in some hospital bed.

But if the prospect of a better universe was so obvious, and if the opportunity presented itself, did I not have a moral duty to try?

"Okay, sure," I said. I'm pretty sure my reply came across as rather sheepish, but there it was. The cards were on the table.

Then I blinked. At least I think I blinked. If I did then I blinked more deeply and for longer than I normally do. And when I woke up – opened my eyes, or whatever you would have called that – there was a sound in the air that I had not heard before. It was like a hum, or perhaps a loud whisper. It was somehow distinctly human, though I had never heard any human utter a noise like it.

Just as I was trying to understand the noise, God abruptly stood up and said, "Let's go for a walk."

As we left the tranquil café for the bustling city street the whisper in the air remained steady. It almost seemed to exist only in my mind because I could not figure out what was causing it. Inside the café, outside the café, it remained constant.

"This is now your world," God declared. "It is a parallel universe. You get to decide how you would like to change it. We will meet once a year at this café and you will tell me what you would like to change. I will make the changes for you, exactly as you ask. The following year I will return and see what further changes you would like to make.

"Nobody can see you, nor can they see me. They cannot hear you, smell you or in any way know that you are here. But you can see, hear and feel them. That sound in your head is easiest to describe as a muffled version of the thoughts of every human. Think of it as the emotional temperature of humanity. You will understand better with time; eventually you will learn to feel what it means.

"What would you like to change?"

This had to be some kind of dream. I must still be lying in the hospital. I was sure I had died, but there was no way this could be real.

Still, just in case it was...

What change to make? I could ask for it all at once, but that seemed foolhardy. If this was really the afterlife then I had all the time I wanted. If this was a hallucination then it didn't really matter either way. Still, start small.

"Eliminate pain," I said. Not too big just yet; baby steps. I wanted to start small and work my up from there. "I don't want any human or any animal to ever experience pain again."

God had remained relatively stoic through most of our conversation, but at that moment he had a look in his eyes that almost hinted of fear or horror. Was he concerned that somebody had discovered his secret? Horrified that humanity knew better than him?

That seemed unlikely, but it seemed ridiculous that he would fear the results of my request. Pain is the single greatest problem we face. We can eliminate it by popping some pills so why not just get rid of it before pills are ever needed in the first place? It's so obvious.

"One year," he said, his voice quivering slightly.

One year indeed. By then it should be apparent what the next improvement should be. Until then, of course, at least these people could start to enjoy their freedom from pain.

With that God vanished.

Perfect World – No Pain

So it was just me and my world.

I stood on the street and looked around. Nothing seemed to have changed. People were still walking around, talking to each other; cars were driving; the general bustle of life proceeded as before.

I noticed a young woman trip on the sidewalk as she crossed the street. She steadied herself, stood up, brushed herself – looking a little confused – and continued on her way. Her confusion, I deduced, was due to the total lack of pain. The way she stumbled it was obvious she should have felt something. Instead, nothing. At least no pain.

I wished I could have told her that she could thank me for that, but alas, I was invisible. It would be a difficult year, knowing I had helped so many people in such a fundamentally significant way, but being absolutely unable to share their joy with them.

Through the window to the café I noticed a man spill his hot beverage on his exposed skin. He pulled his hand back as a natural reflex, but paused, again confused. He wiped it off with a napkin, shook his head in disbelief, and went on his way. Another person spared some hardship.

That noise in my head, though, started to change. It was faint at first, but there was something like an ensemble of high-pitched sounds – suspiciously like shrieks, but that couldn't be right – that started filling the background. It began to rise slowly, steadily, forcibly. Simultaneously the general volume of the hum seemed to subside a little bit, which made the high-pitched notes even more stark by contrast. I wondered what that could mean. Nothing around me looked any different.

As I pondered the change I noticed the mother with her fussy children that I had previously seen in the café. They were outside now, across the street waiting for a bus. There were no more sounds of a fussy baby, but the mother was in hysterics. A handful of strangers at the bus station were trying to help her as she kept reaching into her stroller. Was that blood on her hands?

I went over, out of curiosity. Her youngest child, perhaps a year and a half old, was no longer fussing at all, but she had blood all over her hand and in her mouth. She kept looking up at the adults in confusion and her mother was frantically wiping and bandaging.

The mother kept repeating, frantically, "She was just sucking her thumb. Why didn't she stop? Just sucking her thumb." As her mother fumbled with the bandaging I was able to see the child's thumb. It was bloody and mangled. The child had not merely sucked on her thumb, she had chewed right through it! Right down to the bone!

Dear God! How did that happen? Why didn't the poor child stop?

That was very strange. Disgusted by the sight of blood I moved away from the bus stop. The mother and the bystanders around her seemed to have the situation under control. I tried to put the sight out of my mind.

As I wandered down the street I started to notice more and more perplexed faces. Folks would stare at some part of their body they had obviously scratched or bumped, but without the resultant pain. Some of them smiled, others just looked confused.

Sometime later a young boy bicycled by, giving his little bike bell a ring as he passed another person. He was chasing a friend down the street. He was wearing shorts and I could see a gash in his leg with blood streaming down. But the boy had a huge smile on his face as he was clearly deeply engaged in whatever game the two of them were playing. Oblivious to the pain, the boy just pedalled faster and faster, trying to keep up.

I tried to scream to tell him that he was bleeding but I was invisible to him, and silent. A gash as large as the one he had would normally have been immensely painful, but pain was no longer a feature of this world. I had remedied that.

They rounded a corner and were out of sight. It only made sense that he would notice the blood sooner or later, I concluded.

As I wondered what would happen to the boy an ambulance tore past in the other direction. Once it was out of sight I could still hear its sirens. Or was that a siren from another ambulance? Indeed, I could hear another ambulance rushing in some other direction. Once the noise of the ambulances subsided I noticed a siren sound in my own head. The high-pitched shrill continued to grow.

I noticed the trail of blood that the boy on the bicycle had left behind him, so I started to follow it, out of curiosity. How long before the boy would figure it out? I followed it one block. Two. Given the size of the drops on the pavement it struck me that the boy was obviously losing a lot of blood. This could be a problem.

Another block and the drips of blood started getting smaller. And smaller still. I rounded a corner and noticed a small group of people huddled, a bicycle tossed haphazardly several steps away.

I ran over and, to my horror, saw the little boy who had been happily playing just minutes before, blood spewing from his lower leg. The bystanders had bandaged him up as best they could and were on their cell phones.

"His pulse is gone."

"Does anybody know CPR?"

"9-1-1 says there are no more available ambulances."

"Oh, Lord, he's turning blue!"

"He's dead!"

"Don't stop the CPR!"

"It's over! It's over!"

"Shut up, keep trying. They are sending police instead."

"Does he have a wallet? Who are his parents?"

I backed away. How could I stand and watch? I walked back toward the café. I could hear more sirens in the background and the faces of the people around me started growing increasingly confused and concerned. The shrieks in my head were growing louder, ever louder. My pace quickened and I changed course. This way and that I darted through the streets, not really sure where I wanted to go.

It didn't take long before I was sprinting. I ran and ran until I found a bench in a park with virtually nobody around. I had to sit and think. Without people around it should be easier to concentrate.

But the noise! That awful noise in my head had completely changed. It got louder and more feverish with every passing minute. It didn't take long for me to realize what was causing it. Every mother with a child who had chewed through their own thumb. Every child whose friend had just died from what should have been an easily bandaged wound. How many other stories like these are there? I couldn't think because the noise kept growing louder and louder. As if that wasn't enough the ambulance sirens in the distance became an almost incessant background noise as they rushed people to whatever medical aid was available.

I found a place where I could watch the news that night. It was more horrifying than I could ever have imagined in my worst nightmare. Children all over the planet were dying from unintentional self-inflicted wounds. Youth, adults and the elderly were being permanently disfigured or killed from what should have been easily remedied injuries that they were simply unaware of. Every hospital was turning people away. Morgues were overflowing, especially with the very young; those who did not yet understand the limits of the human body.

The news reporters were talking about something called "congenital insensitivity to pain," a known, but extremely rare, disease. Few children born with this disease survive to adulthood. Those who do virtually always die young and heavily disfigured. It is a horrifying condition that is a curse to any who have it.

I had just stricken the entire human race with this disease!

I screamed out to God to get his attention. I demanded he return immediately. But I recalled what he had promised.

"One year."

It had been only a few hours since he left and already I was on the brink of insanity. I had to last an entire year? Would the human race last that long?

Part of being dead, it turns out, is that one no longer needs to sleep. As if having to watch the horror unfolding during the day was not enough, I had all night to think about what I had done as the sun rose on another part of the planet to bring the bad news of their new condition to another segment of the human race. That shrill horror I heard in my head kept rising, rising, over the course of those first 24 hours.

However, as the days passed the shrill tone in my head eventually faded. The nightly news never stopped covering the story so I was kept well aware of the results of my "improvement" to the human condition. The subsiding shrill was accompanied by a general reduction in the hum I heard. The reason became apparent on the street as well. What was a bustling community of activity became, with time, a very quiet neighbourhood. People stayed at home and participated in as little as they could in order to avoid the possibility of harming themselves. Recreational sports? Gone.

Driving? Much slower and much less frequent. Through the advice of medical experts people eventually learned the "30-second self-exam." In less than a minute they could quickly check the state of their body – a service that pain previously provided, unconsciously, in milliseconds.

Another aspect of the silence was an apparent sense of resignation. Disfigurement and death became far more commonplace. By the time most people with diseases (cancer, heart attack, so many others) became aware that something was wrong, they were far beyond any hope of being cured. The pain that used to serve as an early warning system for many curable illnesses was completely absent. And disease spread rampantly. When a person used to be able to feel a common cold coming on and stay home, they now went out in public, oblivious of their contagious nature. And the common cold was by far the least of their concerns when it came to contagious diseases that began to take over the human race.

Further reason to lock oneself indoors. Further reason to abandon the streets. People became increasingly isolated. Very few people met over coffee. Almost nobody took the bus. Public gatherings of almost every kind (movies, concerts, festivals) were cancelled due to lack of interest.

Not surprisingly, the entire economic system took a major hit. Entire industries shut down almost overnight due to lack of customers. Other industries, those with even a hint of danger to the workers, shut down simply because there were too few employees willing to take the risks. Fear had gripped the entire human race and in many ways civilization itself began to slowly unwind.

People still needed to eat, though. They still needed to pay the bills. These needs drove what little industrial machinery remained. Despite the risks, it was better than starving to death.

But many did starve. Without the ability to feel pain they had no idea they were hungry and, of course, no idea they were dying of starvation. Even though they lacked energy near the end, and eventually just slipped away due to lack of nourishment, it was not as though death was in the least bit agonizing. I had complained to God about the starving kids in Africa that he didn't seem to care about, and now I had introduced far more death into the world than previously existed. Yet, they died pain-free. Was that an improvement? It seemed like a pitiful victory.

Perhaps most disturbingly, suicides were increasingly common. Better the devil you know than the devil you don't, seemed to be the thinking.

I kept wondering if this was just an initial state of shock and if the human race would eventually settle into a new equilibrium. Weeks passed. Months passed. It was just more and more of the same. Fear. Death.

Broken shells of human bodies walked the street in a constant state of fear.

The entire time – day in and day out – I watched it all. Never sleeping, always hearing that cursed noise in my head that continuously reminded me that humanity had moved from a steady hum of activity to a virtually imperceptible buzz combined with a ceaseless shrill that did, eventually, reach an equilibrium. The tone was just high enough to serve as a constant reminder of what I had done but not quite so shrill as it was at first, which would have driven me completely mad.

And mad I nearly was until one day I found myself sitting in the café again, sipping my iced capp, God across the table from me. But the world had changed. It was back to normal. I realized I was no longer in my world but his. Though it was momentary, I immediately soaked in the reprieve.

I was in no rush to go back.

Perfect World – No Harm

"Bring back the pain!" I demanded.

"The intent of all this is to provide you with the chance to make the world a better place. If I bring it back then there has been no progress," he replied.

"Just bring it back!" I insisted.

"I will, I will." He calmly thumbed his cup once again. "So what change would you like to make in its place?"

I wanted so desperately to bring things back to the way they were before, but I saw his point. His world, the world I was used to, was still less than perfect. Something could be done. Some kind of improvement could be made. If getting rid of pain wasn't the answer, what was? I wanted to find a quick answer but I realized that my urgency last time around had caused some – shall we say – unintended consequences.

"Can you give me a minute?" I asked.

"That's a very good idea," he replied. His tone was not the least bit condescending or derogatory. He was very generous through all this. "I'll wait outside; find me when you are ready."

Losing the pain, it turned out, was a very bad idea. Why? Because pain lets us know when we have hurt ourselves. It helps kids learn how to safely interact with the world, and makes sure grown-ups are aware when something is wrong with their body. It is an alarm system to protect us against the dangers of life.

Perhaps therein lay the solution; what if there were no dangers? What if nothing could harm the human body? No injuries. No disease. No death. If the possibility of harm was eliminated that would seem to cut closer to the root of the human predicament. After all, isn't that what Heaven is supposed to be like?

Did I want him to get rid of the possibility of harm and bring back the reality of pain? Without any possibility of harm, though, pain would be superfluous. What would be the point of feeling pain when I stubbed my toe if my toe could not possibly be harmed? No, we have no need for pain if we cannot be harmed. It seemed better to keep the pain away but also eliminate the possibility of harm.

It was far more ambitious than my first request. Vastly more ambitious. It seemed so obvious now; I had been too short-sighted and simplistic in my initial change. This only seemed ambitious because I had initially been too timid.

I rose from my seat and wandered out the door. For some reason my steps were still a little hesitant. Much was at stake. So many people.

"Okay, let's keep it so there is no pain, but make it so that they are unable to be harmed," I said, somewhat sheepishly.

"Invincible?" God asked. When he said it like that it sounded kind of silly.

"Yeah, I suppose," I humbly offered in reply.

There was a hint of resignation in his eye, but nothing like the quivering anxiety last time we'd met.

"One year," he said.

My next blink – if it was a blink – brought me back to my world. I hardly wanted to call it home, but I suppose it kind of was. The café was behind me, the bus stop in front, across the street.

And the noise in my head – much quieter. Timid. When I first arrived in God's world I didn't realize just how much I missed the steady hum over this faint whisper.

The street was so sparse; hardly a person ventured outdoors in the past year. To the few wandering the street I paid careful attention, darting my glance this way and that. Nothing.

I suppose if I would have thought about it I would have realized that any effects from this change were going to be very slowly realized. Humanity had become so terrified of the prospect of injury that they rarely risked anything for fear of an undetected mishap. With their overzealous caution it would take time for them to realize something had changed.

It would take time, but apparently not very much time. On the evening news that night was a story that was being covered by every major news outlet. Absolutely no new admissions at any hospital anywhere on the planet that entire day! Of course the fine print was a little different; people were still so paranoid that they continued to frequent the hospital – just in case – but of all the folks who visited the hospital not one of them actually had something wrong with them.

Over the next days and weeks it got better. Every diseased patient was discharged. Cured!

During this process the noise in my head shifted once again. The high-pitched shrill in the background rapidly subsided. For the first time in a year I was able to rest, really rest. I could feel my emotional state improving as I felt the anxiety of humanity subside.

Finally, we had arrived.

I saw people start coming back out of their houses again. The street filled up with bustling activity again. It was nice to see the city come back to life. Without any of the previous threats that society was accustomed to fearing – murder, rape, gangs and so on – no alley was off limits, no part of town was to be avoided.

But the news was not all good. Without the need for any medical intervention the entire medical industry collapsed. Doctors, nurses, porters, paramedics, pharmaceuticals, hospitals, dentists. Gone, overnight. That was a tough blow to a large part of the economy, of course, but there was still plenty of activity going on; there would be other lines of work. It seemed like a relatively small price to pay.

There was still plenty of work, but it turned out people weren't going to work. This became the highlight of the news for some time. Employees, especially those in blue-collar line of work, started demanding more holidays and fewer hours. They were willing to sacrifice their pay to get it. Eventually they just quit and walked away, even with all those perks.

The buzz at the coffee shop explained their motivation. Starvation was no longer a concern. Neither was housing. If they didn't pay the bills they wouldn't have heat. So what? It's not like they could freeze to death during the winter. No electricity. That's fine, what would they need that for, air conditioning? They could neither feel the discomfort of cold and heat nor could their health be threatened by it. And they neither felt the discomfort of hunger nor could they starve to death.

Without some motivation to keep going to work, large segments of society demanded less and less work, and many more stopped going altogether. Many lost their houses because they wouldn't pay the bills, but they weren't bothered. They just drove to their favourite vacation destination and settled there, many of them living on the beach.

Indeed, leisure time became the primary focus of many people. Motorbikes were all the rage again, especially among those who were formerly concerned with injury. Protective clothing and helmets were nowhere to be found. Sports were back in vogue. All kinds of daring extreme sports suddenly hit the mainstream in ways they never had before. Skydiving without a parachute (especially over jagged rocky mountains) became a pastime for the very extreme daredevils.

Far less work and far more leisure. No pain and no harm. No fear. Truly, it seemed, I had made it.

But something was changing. The noise in my head that had finally taken a tone of bustling activity started growing quieter by the day. The problem with all the leisure, it turned out, was that it depended on a functioning economic system. With time the economy had pretty much collapsed entirely. What would motivate anybody to spend forty hours each week in the office or the factory if they didn't need to eat, clothe or house themselves?

But some people really did want to work. For many people it was not a matter of self-interest that drove their vocational choices (doctors were one example) but a passion for their vocation itself. The problem, though, is that every vocation is intimately connected to every other vocation. The doctor cannot operate on a patient unless there is a building within which to operate, electricity running the building, a company that has manufactured the instruments for surgery, and so much more. Each of those vocations is intimately tied to many other vocations. The company that manufactures surgical instruments relies on another company that provides the raw metal necessary to make the instruments, and that company relies on another company to dig it out of the ground before it is processed. They all rely on the energy industries to fuel the entire economy, governments to keep the rules of the system fair, and so many other players in the interconnected system.

The reality is that many people went to work for the love of their jobs, but when too many people decided that work was simply no longer a worthy end in itself, the economy collapsed. With the rug pulled out from under them, those who loved their jobs lost them through no choice of their own. By comparison, the dirty thirties looked like the swinging twenties.

But at least nobody suffered, even if they no longer had jobs to go to. Leisure time was the defining feature of humanity, at least for those who still had fuel. Once the fuel pumps dried up then travel ground to a near halt. People would still pedal-bike, of course, until their bikes needed repair. With no supplies for repair, and very few bike repair specialists willing to work just for the love of it, most bikes ended up lying in the ditch. People would still walk, until their shoes wore out.

Broken windows, creaky doors, rusted cars, unkempt lawns: these were the fixtures of this world. With a collapsed economy, no reason to work, and the pursuit of beauty so obviously futile given the overwhelming forces acting against it, civilization slipped into utter disarray.

Eventually even extreme sports lost their appeal. Skydiving became impossible anyway due to lack of fuel and functional aircraft, but people tired of it. The thrill of danger is appealing only as long as the danger is real. People would still go for walks and meet for coffee, but it was all just to pass the time. Most of the time when people would meet for coffee they would sit across the table from each other in silence. What was there to talk about?

How is work going? It isn't.

Did you see the game last night? There was no game.

How are your kids doing in school? The schools were shut down due to lack of supplies and, frankly, any reason to be educated.

How was your weekend? Exactly the same as my week.

Time lost all meaning, seasons were irrelevant, there was no work, eventually no leisure, no news, no emails, no mail, no reason to get up in the morning and no reason to go to sleep at night.

In a very unexpected turn of events, relationships themselves lost all meaning and simply fizzled. Friends didn't bother talking to each other and hardly exchanged glances if they wandered by each other on the street. Spouses went wherever they felt like going; not that they were mad at each other, just that the marriage relationship lost any significance. Parents left their children completely unattended. After all, it's not like they could go hungry or die. What did they have to offer them?

Previously, people would cower in their homes for fear of leaving and becoming accidentally injured; now people would settle absolutely anywhere. Personal property meant nothing because they had no reason to go back "home." It's not like it was going to protect them from the elements. Half of their stuff was broken and could not be replaced (not that it needed to be).

Rather, people just slumped on benches. They fell asleep on their lawns. Some would wander aimlessly, literally in circles around the same city block, just so they had something to do.

Some people would attempt suicide. I couldn't remember how many times I saw people dangling from bridges at the end of a home-made noose. Of course they never died; I'd made that impossible. Sometimes another person would release them after some time, but I think the longest I saw a person hanging was about three weeks. She appeared to be in her teens, her clothes mostly tattered, her hair dishevelled and the look on her face quintessentially apathetic about the whole thing. She wasn't the least bit bothered by dangling from a bridge and I'm pretty sure I saw her hanging, again, about a month later. I guess it gave her something to do.

I remember a man, probably in his sixties, who once stood outside in a snow storm, stark naked, arms extended as he faced into the wind. He had a long beard (very few men bothered to shave anymore, even if they had a functional razor) and was tall and scraggly. He must have stood there for three or four hours. He finally went inside. I remember him saying to his wife he could feel that the temperature was cold, but he did not feel cold. She was not the least bit bothered that her husband had been exposing himself to the neighbours, nor that he was standing outside in a blizzard. The only reason most people stayed indoors when the weather was violent was because it took too much energy to get anywhere. Some would still venture out if they felt like staring at something other than their wall for a while. They would go to a coffee shop, or the old museum, and stare at something else, just to pass the time.

The noise in my head was virtually silent. The hum of activity – the soul of humanity, so it seemed – had subsided to a faint lull that I could only really hear on a calm day in a secluded corner.

What had happened? Nobody was happy. They weren't pursing any of the leisure activities they absolutely loved previously. They had no work to go to, nor any reason to go. They had no purpose, no goals, no meaning to life. Physically I had protected them from harm, but I had not considered their emotional state. They had nothing good to feel. They just "existed." They needed to be happy!

I began to think ahead. The one-year mark must have been coming up soon (nobody kept the time or the seasons anymore) so I began to think about what had to change next.

The problem with all of this is that people were bored. They weren't happy. It's not as though they were incapable of feeling happy, but they were not. That was the problem, right? It must have been.

I started wondering how to recreate some of the features of the world I was used to. Stuff like work, for instance, which obviously played a huge role in what it meant to be human. How could we inspire people to go back to work? How could we reignite the economy so people could have the resources to do what they loved to do, and feel the pleasure they previously felt? The need to feed themselves, for fear of the consequences of not feeding themselves, turned out to be the underlying inspiration to work in the old order of things.

But then it occurred to me that I needed to fundamentally shift my paradigm. I was thinking of how to recreate the world we had come from. I was trying to imagine how one might derive pleasure from a specific frame of reference for what "pleasure" looked like. The pleasure I had in mind was tied to a need, a weakness of humanity. Instead, humanity needed to remain free from these needs and limitations and simply experience bliss. I was going about this all wrong!

As a materialist I had learned that all human experiences are reducible to activity in the brain. True happiness did not necessarily need to be tied to any event in the world around us – any sporting event, any concert, work, leisure or even sexuality. These were merely means to an end. The end goal, itself, was pleasure stimulation of our neurons. We could derive pleasure through our visual cortex, our audio cortex, through pleasure sensors all over the body, but in the end they all produced the same physical processes in the brain with or without external stimulation.

Whereas God's world was all about relying on the external, physical world to stimulate those senses, if all those senses were effortlessly stimulated automatically that same end would be realized but without all the trouble and difficulty associated with the world I used to know. In fact – I was growing ambitious now! – it should be possible to vastly increase the pleasure humanity experiences well beyond the meagre limits inherent in God's design of the world. By relying on external stimuli there is only so much pleasure we could possibly derive; by causing stimulation directly in the brain the possibilities were endless! This would be a dreamworld.

Again, I tried as hard as I could to contemplate any ways in which my plan might go awry. I couldn't imagine any, and I felt a little more confident since seeing the results of this second round of improvements. Though this present state of affairs was hardly ideal, it was a far cry from the obvious (in hindsight) mistake I had made the first time around. No, it would seem I was on the right track. Armed with my scientific knowledge of human physiology, and having had time to reflect on it, I waited for our annual coffee.

When the time came I still found myself amazed to suddenly, instantly, be back in the café in God's world. It always surprised me, even when I knew the time was coming up.

The noise in my head when I returned to God's world was almost deafening. I had grown so accustomed to the silence that the hum sounded like an alarm. The noises in the café were also uncomfortably loud, though it was all just the standard noises of conversations, cash registers, coffee makers, cars outside and so on. After a moment I realized the noises both in my head and in the café around me were as they had always been. I had just grown used to silence in my world.

Once I grew used to the noise of God's world I realized that I had kind of missed it all along.

Perfect world – All Pleasure

"Have you given it some thought this time?" God asked. As always he was graciously treating me as his equal, knowing full well that I had reflected on this for several weeks now. Or maybe several months. I could not tell the time in my world.

"Yes," I said with greater confidence than last year.

He thumbed his cup and looked at me, expectantly.

"They need to feel happy. I want you to set it up so all of their pleasure sensors are completely stimulated, all the time."

He looked back at his cup. He took one last sip and as he did I unquestionably saw a tear slide down his cheek.

"One year."

Another blink and I was home. It was so quiet. Deadly quiet. It was the kind of silence that made the slightest breeze sound like a gale; a single leaf dancing along the ground sounded like a child dragging a chair through the kitchen.

In fact, it was quieter than when I had left. At first I assumed my ears were simply readjusting from the noise of God's world, but after a while I realized it was not my ears. Indeed, even the noise in my head was almost completely silenced.

Never had the impact been so sudden. What happened? I wandered around for a few minutes and it became apparent almost immediately. Wherever they had been at the moment that God had graciously granted my request is exactly the location they were now. Nobody moved. If they were sitting, they remained seated. If standing, there they stood. I went up to person after person and it was the same in each of them. Their eyes were fixed off in infinity, mouth gaping open; a slight smirk sometimes marked the corner of their lips. Like statues they remained absolutely motionless, completely internalized by their state of perpetual pleasure.

They did not seem to have any awareness at all of the world around them. Sometimes a person who was standing might get nudged by a breeze and would sit down. Every once in a while a person who was sitting would lie down. It took a few days (or was it months?) but eventually most of the people lay down.

Winter came and went. People were buried under a pile of snow, oblivious. Soaked in rain, showered in sunlight, none of it mattered.

Indeed, nothing mattered. With their every pleasure sensor perpetually stimulated without any interaction with the world outside of their own mind, why bother interacting with anything else? As I thought about this state of affairs I realized that this was the ultimate drug, more potent than anything humans had ever created. No crash, no adverse side effects, perfect euphoria one hundred percent of the time. But why do people use drugs? To escape reality. To escape pain. Rather than choosing to leave reality, though, the human experience that I had created (though to call their present state an "experience" was a generous inaccuracy) essentially forced every single human to unplug from reality and implode into themselves. I had created a world of perpetual junkies, paralyzed by their permanently imposed "high."

I had created the perfect set of ingredients for individual humans to completely cut themselves off from every other human. Humanity was dead, and individual humans were reduced to egocentric shadows.

Gone were the young couples holding hands. Gone were the boys playing with their dogs. Gone were little girls flying kites. Gone were elderly couples enjoying a coffee on the porch. Gone were the young entrepreneurs setting up little cafés such as the one in which God and I had shared several drinks.

Never again would there be a buzz of conversation in the air. No more surprise parties. No more piano recitals. No more creative ways for a young man to pop the question on a jumbotron at a baseball game. No more wedding photos. No more cries of a newborn as that same nervous young man cuts the umbilical cord. No more first bike rides and scraped elbows to kiss better. No more bedtime stories. No more first dates and first kisses. No more walking the bride down the aisle. No more grandkids and retirement.

No husband would ever buy his wife flowers again, or surprise her with chocolates at work. No grandmother would ever take her grandkids to the parade. No more men would dress up as clowns or as Santa Claus to get a laugh out of the young children.

Where were the scientists? Where were the doctors? Would people in this state ever build pyramids, dams or the Great Wall of China? Would they ever master flight or land a man on the moon? Would any of them ever become Michelangelo, Handel or Shakespeare?

Eventually I found myself back in the café where God and I always met. I sat myself down in the chair I always ended up in whenever I blinked. There was nothing to see in this world. Nothing ever happened, so I had nothing to watch. Though the weather came and went, humanity itself was a perfectly stagnant species of absolute inactivity. The owner of the café was seated just behind the counter, head slightly cocked to one side, drool on his cheek.

Was it worth it? Nobody suffered. Nobody cried. There was neither fear nor horror. No death. In one twisted sense this was exactly what I always said God should do. However, it turns out that not only is there nothing horrible, there is nothing good; really, there is nothing at all. No humans ever set goals. No humans ever accomplished anything. No humans ever engaged the rest of the world, took care of themselves, or were even aware of those around them. Each individual was in a state of perfect autonomy.

Clearly something magnificent had been lost, but something else had been gained. Hadn't it? Maybe they didn't have anything to look forward to, or any reason to love one another, but no human suffered. No human would ever be murdered, or die in a car crash. Nobody would ever be traumatized by rape. No little children would ever be abducted, the family mourning their loss for years. No serial killers. No terror bombings. No warlords. No genocides. No droughts and famines leading to thousands of starving children. No diseases eating unsuspecting humans from the inside out. No holocausts. No nuclear wars. Surely this was something good: a world without suffering, fear and mourning. It was good, wasn't it? At least in one sense it had to be.

But God cried. I remember seeing the tear sliding down his cheek. He must have seen this coming and it bothered him. There is no suffering, but there is also no flourishing. Is the elimination of flourishing too great a price to pay just to get rid of suffering? Part of me wanted to yell out, indignantly, "Hell, NO!" because suffering was so great a tragedy. But part of me looked around at these shells of humans, totally devoid of suffering of any kind, and I pitied them almost more than I ever pitied those starving children in Africa that I would see on those TV ads.

Much that was horrible was now gone, but much that was beautiful was equally lost. Why was that? It didn't make sense. Why would the good disappear with the bad? I could not make sense of it. Surely there had to be a way to separate the two. Perhaps I did not have the answer, but surely God could make it happen! If anybody could, it would be him. He can do anything, right?

Anything at all. He could make a world with doctors but without murderers. He could make a world of lovers without rapists. He could make a world with noble presidents without warlords. Couldn't he? Isn't that what Heaven's all about? Why couldn't this world be Heaven? What was stopping it?

What about the economic collapse? That happened because people chose not to go to work. Without the proper motivation – inspired by the necessity of self-preservation – some people refused. But others delighted in their work. Why would some people love their jobs and others do their work only because they have to? Could God not impose in a person the inherent yearning to work? Could he not create beings who automatically loved to work and could not possibly dislike work? Forced love? Is the concept even meaningful? If he could make people love their work then he could create a world where everybody loved each other and nobody hated. What could possibly prevent him? Isn't that the very essence of omnipotence: that nothing at all is impossible for God?

Perhaps there are limits to omnipotence. God told me that he would meet me again in another year. Could he have lied? It would seem that he could not lie; if God is really as good as they say he is, he would tell the truth. But does that make him less than omnipotent or does that just make him consistent in his omnipotence? If his omnipotence is limited in that sense, perhaps it is limited in other senses too. Perhaps he cannot create the "perfect" world.

So many questions, but eventually it became clear to me that I had wasted too much time thinking about these paradoxes. Or had I? Again I recalled that time meant very little here, so perhaps I had only been pondering them for a few days. No, I was sure it had been weeks. I think.

Anyway, the biggest question remained: what next? At some point I would be transported from this seat in this café to the corresponding seat in the corresponding café in God's world. He would want to know what was next. How would I improve on the world? What would I ask for next? It seemed as though the road I had gone down was probably not ideal, but what was the alternative?

I started from scratch in my mind. I wanted a world where pleasure was not automatic, but had to be earned somehow. How? Not sure, I'll get back to that. I still think disease, death and harm have to go. But without hunger a lot of them never bothered working. Could God just make people want to work? But if they always wanted to work then they wouldn't want to rest and enjoy their leisure time. Maybe he could make them want both, but want their work slightly more than leisure.

Forced desires? That didn't seem feasible. If he could do that he could just force everybody to love him and love one another. As an atheist on earth I cherished my freedom to choose whether to believe in God or reject him, love him or hate him. Would I now strip humanity of the freedom I held so dear? Was that the only solution?

Could they be free, but inevitably choose right? No, that was no different than forced love. Was it?

I was getting distracted. Back on track. Okay, so they have to choose to work. Some of them loved their work. Could all work be inherently delightful? It's hard to imagine every single blue-collar job being inherently delightful. Furthermore, I just don't think it is within humanity's nature to always love what is inherently lovable. I recalled asking a friend – a highly successful engineer – what he would do if money were no object, and he told me he would probably just flip burgers. Really? How could he not love his work, just for the wonder of engineering?

No, many forms of work are already wonderful in themselves, but people choose their attitudes more often than not. Many choose not to like their vocations, just as they choose not to like other people and, like me, they choose to reject God himself. Now that I've met him he didn't seem like such a horrible guy, though I'd still love to ask him about all those laws in Leviticus.

So people cannot be forced to freely choose what they ought to do. They need some kind of motivation. Unfortunately, that motivation sometimes needs to be the possibility of some kind of personal harm. Okay, so what if it were just a little bit harmful but not entirely deadly? Just harmful enough to hurt, but not enough to kill them.

What have I done?! Am I seriously considering reintroducing pain and harm into the world? Did it have to come to that? If I followed this line of reasoning death would suddenly sound like a pretty good idea.

Then it occurred to me! The mistake I had been making all along! I had been trying to tell God what to do without asking him why he set things up the way he did. Here I was in an absolutely unique position to actually ask him about his reasons and I never bothered! I had been too busy demanding this change and that; not once had I asked him to explain his side of the story.

This was not me admitting that God was right! By no means! Surely there are ways to make the world better than he did it. It seems so remarkably easy to imagine a better world than the one God created but I had to admit that finding that better world was proving more difficult than I had originally imagined. Instead of starting from scratch and making massive wholesale changes, I would spend some time understanding God's reasons for setting things up as he did and then I would be in a vastly better position to figure out where the improvements lay.

That was it. I would not make any further changes until I had discussed the issue with him and listened to his perspective. My mind was made up.

Now I just waited. And waited. In a world devoid of any activity, any progress, any relationships, any work – anything other than the implosion of the human race into irrelevant, meaningless self-absorbed breathing-corpses – there is nothing else to do but wait.

I didn't know when, but eventually one of these times I would blink and be brought back to reality, or a version of reality that it turns out I missed. Already I was starting to crave the noise, the buzz. It all meant something. As ugly as parts of God's reality were, it was at least interesting. Meaningful.

One of these days.

One of these blinks.

I waited in silence, utterly alone. Waiting to ask God some key questions so I could solve the mystery. Where is utopia? How does one create the perfect world?

Section 3

Real life

The Annals of Facebook

When Denise first arrived in the hospital I was in a bit of a state of disarray, to put it mildly. I just knew that I had to tell people what was going on and ask for prayer. Not sure how best to raise awareness of what happened, I put a simple post on Facebook. I did an update later, but I never really intended to do much after that. However, I soon found out that dozens, hundreds and eventually quite likely over a thousand people – some of them were perfect strangers – were aware of our family's crisis, and that they were eagerly pinned to my Facebook account to receive updates. My Facebook updates became a steady stream of news during this period.

A lot happened prior to my first Facebook status update. Here's a rough outline with approximate times, though I honestly wasn't watching the clock.

11:10 – collapse, discovered by co-workers, CPR started, 9-1-1 called.

11:25 – I got a phone call at home. The Fireman asked a bunch of questions about Denise's condition and medications then told me to stay at home for the time being, he would call back later. I did not know the severity of the situation at this time. He never did call back so part of me assumed the situation had been resolved.

12:00 – I dropped the kids off at school for the afternoon and took the initiative to go to Denise's school to follow up.

12:25 – Arrived at school, was told to go to hospital. Still no real sense of the severity of the situation. Her colleagues were too stunned to explain anything.

12:45 – Arrived at hospital, was greeted by social worker. Denise's mom also arrived. Eventually got to see Denise. Then I understood the severity of the situation.

1:30 – Denise relocated to CICU and the gradual road to recovery began. After that I had the wherewithal to contact the rest of the world.

Below are all the Facebook updates I provided that were relevant to Denise's situation. I have made only minor corrections; what you see is pretty much what I posted.

(Subsequent to this event I deactivated my original account for completely unrelated reasons, in case you try to find the originals on Facebook.)

April 16

4:36 p.m.[28]

My wife is in ER. The situation is very serious. Prayers appreciated. Will update more when I'm at a computer.

April 17

3:28 a.m.

Some more details (from a Blackberry). Denise has always had a heart problem. Typically not symptomatic. She was found unconscious at work Tue around 11:15 a.m. EMS worked on her and transferred her to hospital. Some time later they got her heart to work on its own. She was transferred to Cardiac ICU. They put her in a medicated ""coma"" and cooled her body temp. I guess that gives her brain a better shot at recovering from O2 deprivation. On Wednesday night we'll have a better idea of the long-term prognosis.

Many thanks for prayers but we're not through this yet. That's all for now, it's 3 a.m. and I should try to sleep again.

Visitors are possible, please contact me before you come. I'm not broadcasting my cell on FB so if you don't have it PM me.

BTW, we have the most amazing support structure; couldn't imagine

---

[28] By this time Denise was no longer in ER. My mind wasn't working well, and I was on my Blackberry so I needed to relay the critical message as succinctly as possible.

better for a time like this. So many offers of help! If I do not take you up on it please understand just how many offers we received.

PM me with questions. Cell almost always on.

12:52 p.m.

I'm at home resting and showering so I have access to a computer. It's much easier to type.

Here's a brief rundown of where we are at. Denise is stable but medically paralyzed and in a doctor-controlled hypothermic state. She is unconscious and non-responsive, but this is how the doctors want it to be right now. This is apparently best for aiding the body's recovery from these kinds of things. Around 2:30 p.m. they will start a process that begins with warming her up and then taking her off the medications that are keeping her unconscious. At that point the question is, "What will happen?"

The doctors are not even hazarding a guess. I'm no doctor but I feel I have pieced together a rough picture of the situation and I am not going to sugar coat it. Imagine the worst possible outcome and the best possible outcome; both are fair game as is anything in between. I say that not to attempt to scare anybody but more to keep reminding myself of the gravity of the situation. Hope is only meaningful if it is not false hope. This could turn out really well or really poorly. Be prepared.

Realistically speaking we won't really have any indications at all of what the longer-term picture looks like until this evening and we may not have anything resembling a clear picture for several days. Depending on what happens the recovery process may take much, much longer.

It is not all bad news. We have some miracles to thank God for already. As long as we have known about Denise's heart we have lived with the fear that this would happen at home where nobody would find her for hours. This happened at school. She was seen conscious approximately ten minutes[29] before she was found unconscious so the window between the two was MUCH shorter than it would have been had she dropped the kids off at school, come home and collapsed, unattended for hours.

When the EMS arrived her heart was doing something. She was not flatlined. What her heart was doing was woefully inadequate, obviously, but it was functioning.

The fact that they were able to get her heart working on its own again is another minor miracle. Apparently it is not uncommon for a failure like that

---

[29] Again, details at this point are not always right. At most she was unconscious for ten minutes, but all indications are it was a shorter time than that.

to be the end of the story.[30] Period. Before they put her in the hypothermic state she was breathing on her own (very forced) and her heart was functioning on its own. Both are good signs.

The fact that this happened when she was young is, ironically, a good thing. Youth and general health increase the likelihood of a healthy recovery. If this happened in another ten or twenty years this message might have been worded quite differently.

We are emotionally beat. I'm not even sure if posting this on Facebook is wise but I'm tired and drained and I think many people would like to hear it. I hope I won't regret this. I hope this is not a lapse of good judgment. Please only share as is appropriate, obviously.

Many tears have been shed and many prayers have been said; keep them coming. I do not believe in the power of prayer, I only believe in the power of the one to whom we pray. He brought himself out of a tomb 2,000 years ago and if he can do that (and if he wills to) he can bring Denise out of this. He is able.

I won't have any news until this evening at the earliest and maybe nothing until tomorrow. Again, if you have specific questions or would like to visit, PM me. Visitors are allowed in small quantities and with prior notice.

6:23 p.m.[31]

Slight change of plans. She will warm up this evening and the meds start coming off mostly tomorrow morning. No news until the morning. Maybe midday.

Her cardiac specialist came by and offered some reflections. Generally positive, but cautiously so.

---

[30] Talk about an understatement! As I later found out, it is vastly more likely that a cardiac arrest ends in death than that the victim recovers, unless an AED is immediately on hand, which was not the case in this situation.

[31] I think it was in the hours before this post that I had the most sobering conversation I've ever had with my son who was eight years old at the time. We were in the room with Denise – still completely unconscious and hooked up to innumerable tubes and wires – when Cole asked, "When is mommy coming home?" The natural fatherly instinct is to lie to his face and tell him, "very soon," but he's a smart kid and I was certain he would see through my deception. I was cornered. I had to confess, "I don't know if mommy is coming home." At the time, that was the honest truth. That is one phrase no father should ever have to tell his young child and it haunts me to this day.

9:51 p.m.

Temp back to normal. The med that causes paralysis has been removed. Sedation meds slowly being weaned off with more rapid weaning at 7 a.m. Should expect some kind of results around 8 to 9 a.m. Visitors probably shouldn't come by until late morning or afternoon. Call first (or PM me).

April 18

5:51 a.m.

Good morning. Meds continued to be weaned overnight. She has opened her eyes a couple of times when being moved but nurses said she did not respond with squeezing her hand. Small signs, but good. I saw her eyes twitching (though closed). Heart rate and temperature looking more normal. Still waiting until 7 a.m. when things should really take off.

Nurses are paying very close attention; staff is marvelous here.

I had approximately six hrs of sleep and am functional. More updates as relevant.

6:55 a.m.

She started doing basic response to basic stimuli. Meds continue to drop.

8:05 a.m.

Sedation meds are completely off. Will be in her system for a while yet. Veeeery slowly waking up.

8:45 a.m.

My understanding of the timeline was off. Today we will only have faint hints of the situation. Denise will still be asleep for most of the day. Tomorrow will give a clearer picture but today we will still get to see some activity and progress. And we are seeing gradual progress.

The mood amongst everybody (including medical staff) is cautious optimism. More laughing and smiling than crying today.

Still difficult to watch her. Prayers and encouragement appreciated.

9:50 a.m.

Just got an update from doctor. At this stage in process he says Denise's progress is pretty much as expected. There's still a long road ahead but at least it seems we are roughly where we ought to be on that road.

Still no guess about possible neurological damage. No grounds to guess from just yet.

10:44 a.m.

She just opened her eyes on her own initiative and tried to move her head. Still will not squeeze hand. Was responsive for several minutes and is resting again. Exciting!

3:30 p.m.

Denise moved her hands and feet as instructed by the doctor. Not only can she obviously hear us, she can now control some parts of her body enough to listen to instructions! This is quite exciting to see. She still is in some discomfort, but this is promising.

5:33 p.m.

So just moments ago I was communicating with her. The breathing tube must be horribly uncomfortable. I kept reminding her to try and stay as still as possible. I said, "It must feel awful." She nodded! She's still also trying to move her head. Also fairly certain she was actually looking at me instead of just staring into space.

Good signs.

7:44 p.m.

It's hard to keep up with the progress. It improves by the hour. Smiling, nodding, turning her head, lifting one arm, visually tracking a person, etc. Biggest prayer request right now is the removal of her breathing tube. Necessary evil. Once she is adequately able to breathe on her own it's outta there! Pray that she heals quickly so we can get rid of it quickly!

11:10 p.m.

The paramedics who drove Denise to the hospital stopped by tonight. They just wanted to see how she was doing. It gave us a chance to "interrogate" them (all friendly). At the scene when Denise went down there were both paramedics and fire department. The captain of the fire truck was the guy who called me at home that day. I couldn't give him much info but I could tell him the name of Denise's cardiac specialist. "Oh, her!" he replied. I just assumed first responders were acquainted with specialists like her for this very reason.

Not so. This one individual happened to personally know, on a first name basis, the specific cardiac specialist for the specific woman he was currently trying to save the life of. Out of a city of a million people, what are the odds of getting exactly the right fireman who knew exactly where

Denise's cardiac specialist worked and could immediately get her on the phone to get exactly the cardiac info they needed at that exact moment? Coincidence? I'm skeptical!

That's another little miracle we just learned about tonight. The list continues to grow.

April 19

6:42 a.m.

Uneventful night. She was put back on low dosage of sedation meds because she was very uncomfortable with breathing tube (gee, hard to imagine why?!). She slept through the night. Unfortunately I did not sleep so much. Did not get enough sleep to be properly functional so will go home once Gerry arrives in a bit.

Pray that she can breathe on her own so that the (insert expletive here) breathing tube can come out today. Sedations are being removed as I type so we restart the recovery process right now. Here we go again...

No more updates until I have more rest.

9:14 a.m.

I've been told that perhaps not all my updates are being seen by everybody. I don't know if there's a difference between "timeline" and "status" or whatever other FB features there are that I've been using. Comment among yourselves if anybody can't find all the updates. Sorry if anybody isn't getting all the info.

Off to nap. More updates when I awake.

4:32 p.m.

I've been slow with updates today, sorry. I visited Denise's school and tried to nap (failed). The doctor is sufficiently impressed with her heart progress to have removed more meds. She is half way through breathing test and passing well so far! If this keeps up, the tube could come out. Prayers for sleep right now would be great.

She is very communicative. Hard to explain on Blackberry, will describe another time.

5:26 p.m.

I showed Denise the cards the kids made for her. She smiled as much as she can with the tube in her mouth. Cole came a while later and she tried hard not to gag when he was there but he eventually left because it is somewhat dramatic when she gags. She loved seeing him so tried to keep calm. Sydney is with Colleen at the time. When he left she remained aggravated. My mom finally figured out that she wanted to see Cole again. Sure enough, when he returned she seemed content again. Very special.[32]

6:20 p.m.

Good news and bad news. Bad news is she really wants something very badly and cannot tell us what she wants. We've tried multiple ways to figure it out, no luck. Good news is the energy she is putting into trying to tell us. She is trying to get out of bed! Think about that! Using abs, legs, arms, neck, etc. Full body effort. Also, she's trying to write! We got a pad of paper and a pen and she made some scribbles. Some of them almost looked like letters!

Still waiting on the breathing tube. Possibly another hour or two.

6:53 p.m.

She passed the breathing test with flying colours (per respiratory technician). Current plan is to remove the tube in the morning, perhaps 8 or 9. Pray for a solid night sleep and a good physical assessment by the doctors in the morning.

10:02 p.m.

Last update for the night before I finally get to try and sleep at home for a change.

Progress continues to be made. She was using her tongue to feel some of the finer features of the breathing tube. She is using greater facial expression (raised eyebrows, etc). Respiratory Technician checked back again on her status and reconfirmed that he's very happy with what he sees. It's a very high likelihood (nothing is certain!) that the tube comes out tomorrow morning when the doctors do their rounds about 8 or 9. Again, please pray for a good sleep for her tonight.

As Denise is spending more and more time awake she will have greater and greater influence with respect to how many visitors she has and how often. We will almost certainly have to start limiting the number of folks who come by. Please do feel free to ask us about coordinating a visit but expect that we might get you to wait a few days or so. In fact this weekend (Saturday in particular) will be a little more family-centred as she should be

---

[32] This was a very difficult decision for me. As a husband I wanted to bring the kids in for her benefit. As a father I wanted to keep them out, for their benefit. I still wonder just how traumatized they are to this day because they had to see her in that condition, smiling and gagging.

able to speak again.

Thanks for all the prayers; God is listening and answering in ways we only hoped for.

April 20

8:09 a.m.

As usual I'm a little more eager than the doctors who want to play things safe. They are likely to see her around 9 a.m. but there is still a bit of a process to getting the tube out (paperwork and such). Still, every indication is that it'll come out this morning. Denise keeps trying to talk which is a great sign.

10:24 a.m.

Tube is out!![33]

11:07 a.m.

She talks. Many questions from her. Only whispering at this point. Most common questions are "How did this happen?" "Why can't I go home?" "How long will I be here?" Unfortunately she asks the questions repeatedly about every few minutes.

Prayer requests include the prevention of infections of various kinds and short-term memory improvement. More requests later, I'm sure.

12:20 p.m.

Today is the first time since Tuesday morning that I have really seen my wife. Too many good signs of progress even in the past two hours to remember and share. Might try to summarize later when I'm at a computer.

1:13 p.m.

She's cracking jokes, planning for the future, and she just scolded me. We have Denise back!! The doctor (who is inherently very cautious) gave a rave review of her condition so it's not just my uninformed opinion.

God has chosen to answer our prayers so far in ways none of us could

---

[33] Interesting aside. Sydney's teacher told us later that it was on this day he met the "real" Sydney. She is a fairly outgoing child at home, but for whatever reason the entire school year (even well before this event) she was relatively quiet and almost withdrawn in his class. But her excitement at seeing her mom without the breathing tube flipped a switch in her and she's never been the same at school since. She was finally herself.

have imagined. Pray for patience for Denise on the long road to recovery.

6:18 p.m.

Another prayer item. Denise is understandably frustrated by her circumstances. Just like anybody in a hospital she would really like to go home. Patience and perseverance as well as a peace about the whole situation are needed.

9:10 p.m.

Final update for today. Much progress. She is more coherent, attempting independence (i.e. trying to feed herself), accessing memories, etc. Not holding my breath but short-term memory seems to be improving. Still wants very much to go home and is visibly frustrated with circumstances. Not surprising; who wouldn't be?

She is asleep and I suspect will sleep well. What will tomorrow bring? God only knows, we wait.

April 21

7:19 a.m.

Time for a high-level summary of the situation since I'm at a computer.

Denise's recovery at this point is very good considering her situation when she entered the hospital. Even her doctor was smiling when he shared his glowing report of her progress and he has a very reserved and cautious type of personality. We all know there is a long, difficult and patience-testing road ahead of us but we are just so relieved to be where we are right now.

This is all rather difficult and confusing for Denise, which is absolutely to be expected. When she woke up on Thursday she had no knowledge, at all, of the events of the previous days. From her perspective it must feel like she went to bed one night and woke up connected to tubes, stuck in a hospital and nobody will let her go home. Put yourself in her shoes; I don't think I would be in a particularly good mood in that situation. But she does smile and she does offer some wit and some of her response is related to the medications she has been taking.

The kids and I are getting along alright. The kids were really affected by all this (not to say I wasn't!) and I cannot describe the size of the smile on Cole's face when he found out the breathing tube was out. Sydney was actually playing games of a simple sort with Denise yesterday; just silly kid stuff, hard to describe.

I'm doing alright too. I'm getting just enough sleep to manage and I'm being forced to be an extrovert for a while. For the record, energy drinks are a gift straight from God himself. This is not the best time of life for me, obviously, but I am drawing on a strength far beyond what I possess in myself; Jesus is even more effective than energy drinks!

A couple of logistical notes. People keep asking how they can help. At this point we really are pretty well covered for food, child care, etc. We are so grateful for the support network that sprang into existence the moment the news went out about Denise's situation, and we intend to take advantage of it, but we're not in a position right now to know what that is going to look like in the long term. I would love to see our kids go on more play dates in the weeks to come. Some of you have already had our kids for play dates; thank you. If you would like to take them out to something special now and then, touch base with us. Again, remember that there's a long list of folks so there may be a bit of a waiting game involved.

Meal prep is in overdrive right now, but in a few weeks' time it might be helpful to have some stuff in the freezer. Don't jump on that right now; we'll let you know when it's the right time. Just think ahead and know that we intend to take advantage of your generosity.

I have no idea what the next few weeks are going to look like but I imagine there will come a time when Denise will really delight in having some visitors either in the hospital or as she recovers at home. Plan to come with some kind of activity or something, I think. She likes game, for instance. It's not time for those kinds of visits right now, but we all love her and I understand that folks would like see her and help lift her spirits. That day will come, so think ahead to how you might like to engage with her at that time. As always, contact us before you come and you may have to deal with a little waiting.

This is kind of a silly thing, but I know that many of my new Facebook "friends" only friended me because they wanted to see updates on Denise's progress. Thank you for your concern and involvement in prayer. When the dust settles on this episode please understand that I will not be in the least bit offended when you "unfriend" me. Trust me, my self-confidence rests on something far deeper than buttons clicked at some social media website. When the time comes don't hesitate at all to click that button!

We have so many thank you's to send out for prayer and support, and we are almost certainly going to have more thank you's before this is all done. However I do just want to offer a blanket statement really quickly to say that your involvement in all of this, whether through physical support, emotional support or spiritual support has been very apparent and very appreciated. We are so humbled by all of you coming together and would like to find the right words to thank you, but they all come short. The effects of your support (particularly prayer) are numerous and clearly seen.

Never before in my life have I understood this Psalm in such a literal sense.

Even though I walk through the valley of the shadow of death, I will fear no evil, for you are with me; your rod and your staff, they comfort me. (Psalm 23:4 ESV)

On Tuesday Denise entered the hospital very much in the shadow of death. For her, on that day, this verse was not metaphorical. As was the psalmist, we were comforted both by God and by our friends. You have been the instruments of God, even if you don't know him or accept him. Thank you.

10:17 a.m.

Morning update. Her bed turns into a chair (I absolutely need one of these!) so she's sitting up. She slept okay but remains absolutely exhausted. Still keeps asking about going home. Getting her fine motor control back, slowly. Spirits lifted when she sees pictures of, and cards from, her kids and nieces and nephews.

Given how exhausted she is we are going to be fairly cautious with visitors. If you would like to visit by all means touch base with us, but don't expect to come right away, and expect that this visit will be short.

Still, thrilled with her progress and dealing with the remaining challenges.

7:31 p.m.

Last update of the day. Most of the tubes are gone. More awake time than previous days (though still resting a lot). Fine motor skills improving dramatically; she's feeding herself simple stuff. She's in a new room too; one with a window to the outdoors. When the kids were here she brightened up in ways I cannot describe.

Memory is still an issue, which is probably the biggest prayer item right now. Second biggest would be patience.

April 22

6:12 a.m.

People keep asking about how our family is doing so I'll give a little update on that front. The kids have been staying with my parents and the plan is to continue that into the foreseeable future. They have been amazing through all this. When it first happened they were visibly bothered and also seemingly confused. It's like they didn't even know what questions to ask in order to understand why mommy is lying on the bed sleeping, with tubes and wires going in and out of her mouth, arms and neck. How do you explain that to a child?

Yesterday, though, they were talking with her, sitting on her lap, hugging her, helping feed her (she needed little help) and much more. She is bringing a smile to their faces and they are definitely bringing a smile to her face.

They are off to school this morning and we are making plans to get them plugged back into routine. I think that will help.

I am doing alright. I had a good sleep last night (eight hours, minimum) and I'm eating well enough. I'm still stumped when I try to pray about all this. I totally lack a frame of reference to understand what's going on so I don't know what to say to God. Even something as simple as "thank you" is confusing. I'm a thinker – an analytical kind of guy – so to not understand is strange for me. I suspect, though, that my emotions are not letting me think right now because I have already cried so many tears of sorrow, pain and then joy that if I really thought about this and understood it I would end up bawling for weeks on end and I cannot do that right now. The time for total processing will come, but right now there is work to do.

Out of respect I cannot and will not speak in specific terms about the rest of my family (most are on Facebook, you can ask them yourself) but I think it is safe to say the general theme is an emotional roller coaster, physical exhaustion, but a sense of joy at where we are.

Really what we all need is Shalom – God's peace. That covers physical rest and health, emotional healing, intellectual comprehension of all this (still lacking) and spiritual peace.

I have not been to the hospital yet so I cannot update Denise but I will let you know how last night ended; it is telling. I came back to her room to find her contentedly watching TV with her glasses on. I told her how I was planning on staying a little later and then going home. I wanted to stick around until she was asleep because I was concerned about her waking up in the night and being confused. She looked at me with those "don't treat me like a baby" eyes and told me to go home. She's nothing if not fiercely independent!

She needs to regain control of, and use of, her body. She has much of her fine motor control regained, but not a lot of strength. She has not used her legs in almost a week and has not even tried walking yet.

We have started discussing long-term treatment options for her heart. There are a few options on the table with various strengths and weaknesses. No decision just yet.

Her memory is still an issue. Short-term memory needs a lot of work and it seems that even her long-term memory is a bit spotty within the past one to eight months. She seems to remember some things from about a month ago, but forgets some things from eight months ago. The numbers are just approximate, not precise, and there is no way of mapping out exactly what she does and does not remember.

Anyway, I need to get ready to head to the hospital; I'll update when I arrive. By the way, given her progress I think it's safe to say that updates will be a little more sparse from this point forward. She is doing really well and has regained a lot of her abilities so there comes a point when there is less and less to report.

Thank you all for your prayers and thank God for hearing and answering our prayers in the way we wanted him to. This is one of those times when I definitely didn't want to hear God say, "no." He didn't. He seems to be saying "yes" to everything we ask right now. We always trust his sovereignty and wisdom, but in this case we are thankful that what he wants and what we want happen to coincide.

Prayer items:

- That the kids would continue to process and recover from this event
- That the kids would start to re-engage "normal life" to some extent (school, piano, play dates, etc.)
- That the adults in Denise's life would experience God's Shalom.
- Denise's memory issues, strength and coordination, and that we would make the right choice for her long-term heart treatment.

2:07 p.m.

Funny story. I go in to see if Denise is still sleeping (as I left her) and I find her standing! The physiotherapist showed up and wanted to do a quick initial assessment. She's sitting in a chair for the time being – just fifteen minutes at a time.

Standing!!

9:06 p.m.

Evening update.

First things first, updates will probably be a little slower from this point forward. We are definitely moving away from "crisis" mode into recovery and long-term treatment mode.

As I said earlier, she stood up. This is probably far more psychologically encouraging for the rest of us than actually a major step in her physiological rehabilitation. Still, we accept any encouragement we can get!

She had several significant visits today. The three ladies from her school who took care of the CPR last Tuesday came by. It was a great visit for everybody, though significant for each person in very different ways. She also received a number of cards from her students with the promise that more were on the way.

Some specialists stopped by to discuss rehabilitation and heart treatments, including the physiotherapist, a heart specialist and, much to Denise's delight, a dietician. Why would this delight Denise? Because she can now eat "normal" food which we are more than happy to provide her with. And we will go out of our way to provide her with home-made "normal food" instead of hospital food because hospital food is… um…

Where was I? Oh, yes: other longer-term plans. She will probably be moved to another unit tomorrow. This is another sign that the doctors are very pleased with her status and don't see any need to keep her on the Intensive Care Unit. She will have some more tests done, meet more experts and so forth in the next few days, all of which is aimed at the goal of getting her out of the hospital and significantly reducing the likelihood that she will ever come back under similar circumstances.

I will also start transitioning away from being glued to my blackberry because we are no longer in crisis mode. I have always tried to respond to people immediately, and will generally continue to do so, but there may be times when I just need to shut it off for personal sanity reasons. If you don't get an immediate reply I'm probably not mad at you or anything!

Prayer requests:

- That the doctors would hone in on the right long-term heart treatment plan.
- She is about to start in on various forms of rehabilitation; give her patience and tenacity.

- She is understandably frustrated with her circumstances; she needs patience and enough to occupy her mind and time so she doesn't go crazy. Little kids seem to have the most visible and enduring impact on her (not just her own kids, either!)
- Memory is still an issue.
- That we might figure out the juggling act around visitors. Visitations are not just for Denise's benefit, though she seems to enjoy them, but we need to balance the needs of those who visit with Denise's needs as well. We are not always doing this right.

By the way, I am deeply grateful that the City of Calgary has decided to postpone summer once again. It was nice to see the snow flying while we were stuck indoors anyway.

April 23

8:21 a.m.

We have been sharing the family waiting room with another family whose grandmother was horribly ill. We knew it was terminal. Yesterday they were cycling through, I kid you not, dozens of relatives both close and distant. The family room was a bustling hub of activity as there were so many relatives that they ended up pouring into the hallway as they waited their turn to offer their last farewells. Although it was an inconvenience for our family nobody would dream of saying anything, obviously, given the gravity of their situation.

This morning the family room was empty. The patient's room too. The silence was a sobering reminder that many of these stories do not end like Denise's. I am extra grateful for God's healing as I sit in solitude in the otherwise abandoned waiting room. May that family mourn with peace.

5:35 p.m.

Much to say, stuck with Blackberry! This will be brief, to the point. Went to firehall today and talked with firemen who responded. It was also for their emotional good it turns out. One paramedic said of all the cardiac arrests he has responded to only two have recovered. Denise is one of those. Read elsewhere that only five percent of sudden cardiac arrests survive. Percentage probably higher for younger folks, but still...

Denise had tests today and got a ride in a wheelchair to get there. First time out of her room and she was not in bed when she went. More progress.

Occupational Therapist showed up. Really friendly guy. Gave us some rough numbers of how long she might be in hospital. Not more than two months. That helped Denise.

She gets her ICD implanted tomorrow. Pray for no complications and a successful surgery. Estimated surgery time is 1 p.m.

She's still eager to leave but seems somewhat more content with circumstances. Has started brainstorming trip to tropical destination.

6:04 p.m.

By the way the surgeon doing the ICD (fancy pacemaker) implant did the very first ever such implant in all of Alberta which was the second ever such implant in all of Canada. That was back in the seventies. He's been doing them ever since. Would anybody happen to know a more qualified ICD surgeon? I'm concerned about his qualifications!

April 24

8:23 a.m.

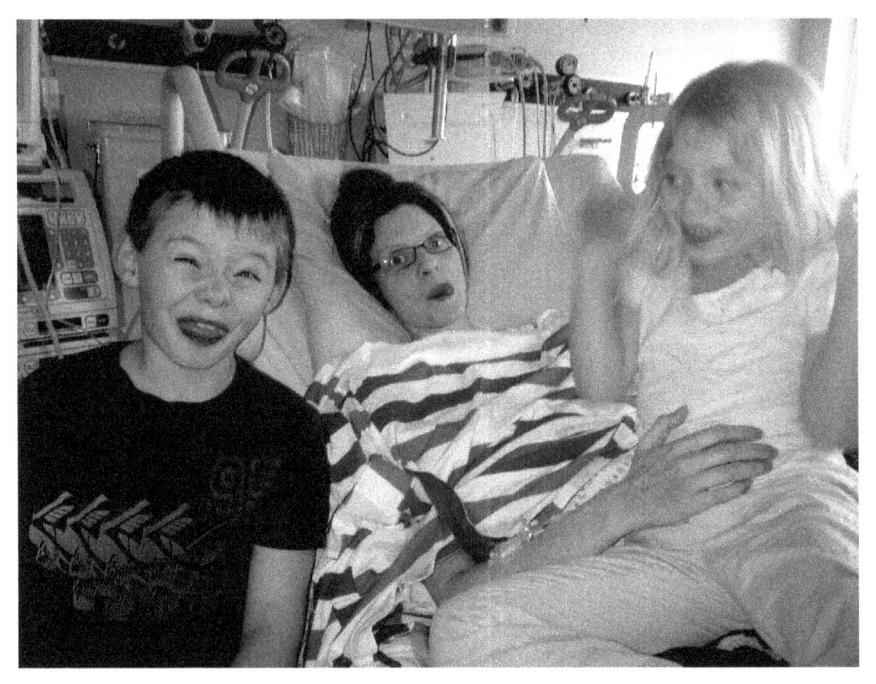

A sight many of us wondered if we would ever see again!

12:21 p.m.

The OT came by again. What a delightful man! He is all smiles, all encouragement, and just an absolutely lovable demeanour while maintaining full professionalism and focus. He did an initial neurological assessment to see what challenges lie ahead and what the program needs to look like to help her recover her functionality. No real surprises.

Denise's surgery is still scheduled for 1 p.m. Pray for a successful surgery without complications.

In general Denise seems to very slowly be improving but there's still a long way to go. She sat up for quite a while the OT interviewed her. Pray for peace; Shalom.

2:46 p.m.

She went in to surgery late, around 2 p.m. No news yet. Will probably see her again around 4 at her new unit.

Another physiotherapist dropped by and did some more testing on Denise. I thought did well, but I'm no expert. She could do just about anything the physiotherapist asked of her which felt encouraging.

Her disappointed demeanour seems to be slowly subsiding but far from disappearing. Not sure how much is due to neurotrauma, how much to circumstances and how much to the fact that her heart issues have always bugged her.

3:31 p.m.

I just had a chance to pray with somebody on the verge of being involved in the decision to pull the plug on their family member. Please join me in giving them a sense of peace for their decision.

Denise is not out of the surgery yet but should be soon. Will post when I have details.

5:09 p.m.

She's out of surgery. Appears all went well. She's now on a longer-term recovery unit with an explicit ban on flowers and anything else aromatic like that. Allergies and all.

She seems to be in decent shape. She was only given a local anaesthetic so the effects are reduced.

8:41 p.m. (This was posted by Denise's mom, Gerry, and I shared the update.)

It is Wednesday and I am home this evening feeling much more calm about our crisis. Denise had her defibrillator/pacemaker put in today and surgery went well, as far as we know. That was a big thing for me. Tomorrow they will program it, take an X-ray, check if the meds are doing the right thing and watch her. I will be able to start to focus more on Monica and her baby that is due. Please pray for my health and strength to keep going, as I must admit I am tired.

April 25

8:59 a.m.

I think we have kind of a low-key day ahead of us. Chest X-ray to ensure the ICD implant went well. Somebody will come up and get it set up "remotely" (through her flesh). OT plans to come by daily. Probably a bit of physio.

Her sore arm appears to be doing well. Pray for good healing from the surgery.

The emotional aspect of healing may be the biggest hurdle at this point. It seems to me that her neurological "bump" has caused a slight shift in her demeanour. I'm sure the neuro-rehab will help out with that, but for now she has more of a frustrated perspective on her situation than she would normally default to. Pray for that, definitely.

2:47 p.m.

A few things of note. Chest X-rays this morning came up good. Doctors are happy with the implant. No signs of infection thus far.

PT and OT both came by. She walked from her bed to another bed to the window and back again. Seemed relatively balanced, etc. PT observed that she's doing better than when she saw her on Monday.

The ICD tech nurse also came by to adjust the settings of the ICD. At one point she said, "you'll feel your heart speed up a bit here" and she clicked a button. She could control the speed of Denise's heart with the click of a button!! Think about it. How cool is that? I know I'm such a tech geek but that totally made me want to get one and figure some way of programming it with an Android IOS or something. Any other nerds out there agree on how cool that is?

She's still down in the dumps but apparently that is not an uncommon reaction to stuff like this. That and memory issues are our biggest struggles at this point. Her heart stuff is pretty much taken care of except for some minor tweaking of her meds.

She has been moved to another room on the unit that is semi-private and she has a window view. I hope that helps. The plan is for her to stay on this unit until Monday or Tuesday when she'll move to the neuro-rehab unit. At that point life should become more predictable and routine until we're out of here. She needs patience and dedication to the work involved. I don't think the latter will be any issue, but the former might just be.

As always thank you so much for your prayers. I have a blog entry coming in which I reflect on prayer with respect to this entire episode. In fact, I have a few blog entries coming up (much to ponder...). Stay tuned.

6:05 p.m.

So I learned something interesting today. As an engineer I have a keen awareness that no systems (especially man-made ones) work to 100% of their expectation. I was curious about Denise's ICD. If her heart enters a dangerous and potentially fatal rhythm and the ICD shocks her, what is the likelihood that it will successfully restore a proper heart rhythm? Surely this is a relevant question given what she has just gone through and the possibility that it might happen again at some point in her life.

I asked three people that question and got pretty much the same answer: virtually 100% certainty. One doctor, speaking off the cuff, said 99.9%. Another doctor said 96 to 98%. The ICD nurse said that the hearts it tends to not work on are those hearts that are dying or too diseased to recover. Denise is certainly not in that category, despite her odd heart rhythms, so we have every reason to believe that if her heart does what it did last Tuesday the ICD will save her life. At least 96% certainty.[34]

I don't know about you, but I will certainly sleep better at night knowing that.

April 26

4:02 p.m.

Busy day! PT and OT visited in the morning. She walked a distance I would estimate at about 40 metres and both PTs said their contribution to her balance and strength was minimal. In other words, she didn't really need a lot of help. OT did a couple of tests to continue narrowing down the

---

[34] In the years that followed the initial event her ICD has saved her life multiple times when her heart slipped back into its deadly failure mode, the same mode that sent her to the hospital. The device is so effective that her heart has only ever required a single shock, and less than a minute later she is up and about as if the whole thing never happened. It is a truly remarkable piece of technology.

neurological issues we'll have to work on. His pleasant demeanour (did I mention how much I love the guy?) is winning her over and she remembers and likes him. That will help the therapy. In terms of what to work on there is the memory, of course, and a few other issues that are hard to describe quickly and probably aren't interesting to most people. I'll skip the details; the long and short of it is that she has work to do but there is still no reason to believe she won't make her way out of the woods eventually.

She was moved to another room again, but this time to a completely private room. Her own bathroom and everything. No hot tub, but I did ask.

She had a shower pretty much all by herself. Once she was clean her entire outlook changed. It's amazing how much that can impact a person.

She got to see her brand-new niece (as of 5 this morning)! How did we get her there? By the wheelchair. Yes, her mobility increases daily and I hope her and I can go on a little "date" sometime soon; just down to the illustrious, and highly recommended, hospital café. I hear the food there is exceptional and the service is award winning.

Everybody is shutting down for the weekend so probably not much to update on until next week. The plan then is to move her to the neuro-rehab unit. Not sure when, exactly; the story changes depending on who you ask.

Prayers are still the usual. Peace, patience and a positive disposition as she recovers. They are continuing to fiddle with her heart meds; may they get the right mix before she is discharged.

Visitors should be a little easier to accommodate over the weekend and next week as she continues to get her energy back. Contact us (myself or Gerry) ahead of time and expect either delays or a short visit depending on how the day has unfolded.

April 27

6:28 a.m.

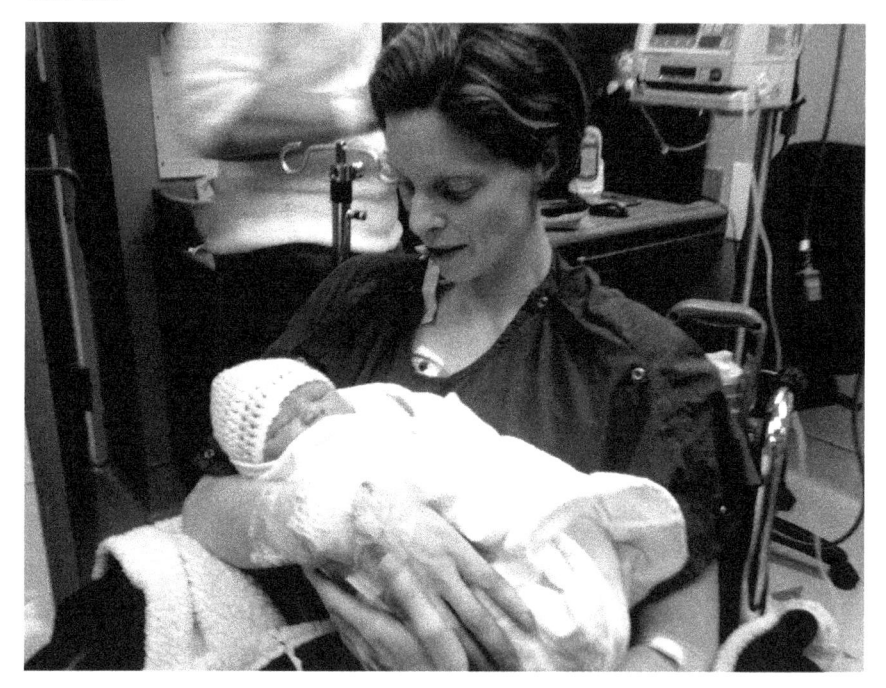

Restored life, new life

Here's a shot of Denise holding her little newborn niece, Isabel. The gift of life comes in many forms.[35]

10:01 a.m.

She woke up in a much better mood this morning. Of course this will be an up and down journey but it is nice to see part of the up side. She had a shower, blow dried her hair and visited Monica and Isabel. Despite her memory issues she never forgets Isabel's name. More guests are coming today; lots on the go, but we are making sure to include downtime in the mix. Hopefully I'll even take her outside for a breath of fresh air.

She had her IV removed and not replaced, and it sounds like she only needs to wear the heart monitor for one more day. She could be completely probe and tube-free tomorrow! That would be exciting for her, I think. She had some clothes brought to her but lacked the energy to put them on yet.

---

[35] As an illustration of her memory issues related to the event, to this day Denise has no recollection of holding Isabel as shown in the photo.

Maybe later today. Bit by bit her life and circumstances in the hospital are approaching "normalcy."

Slow and gradual, but the progress is all in the right direction. Please continue to pray for her brain healing, patience and emotional health.

3:37 p.m.

I cannot describe how magnificent today was. So many excellent experiences but there was one that reduced me to putty. I cannot even type this without crying.

She wanted to go to the Chapel and play piano. I kept my thoughts to myself, but given the fact that she cannot even write a short sentence without misspelling every second or third word I didn't think there was much of a chance in the world that her fingers would have any inkling of what to do with the ivory.[36]

She played. From memory. And guess what song she chose? The lyrics are below for those who don't recognize it in the video. Just read the words and let the full depth of meaning flow over you, especially given her present circumstances. Is there a deeper way to honour God than what Denise did this afternoon? I cannot imagine one. I am put to shame.

She chose that song, she remembered it, and with only a few errors her fingers found their way through the melody. You can imagine why the camera isn't particularly steady.[37] I'll never sing that song the same way again, and it was already a very meaningful one to me.

Blessed be Your name

In the land that is plentiful

Where Your streams of abundance flow

Blessed be Your name

Blessed be Your name

When I'm found in the desert place

Though I walk through the wilderness

---

[36] Later, during therapy, Denise was unable to play the piano. It's as if she (and I) needed that moment of encouragement that day, so she enjoyed a temporary break in her recovery process as God momentarily restored sufficient functionality.

[37] I recorded the event on video and posted to Facebook.

Blessed be Your name

Every blessing You pour out
I'll turn back to praise
When the darkness closes in, Lord
Still I will say

Blessed be the name of the Lord
Blessed be Your name
Blessed be the name of the Lord
Blessed be Your glorious name

Blessed be Your name
When the sun's shining down on me
When the world's 'all as it should be'
Blessed be Your name

Blessed be Your name
On the road marked with suffering
Though there's pain in the offering
Blessed be Your name

Every blessing You pour out
I'll turn back to praise
When the darkness closes in, Lord
Still I will say

Blessed be the name of the Lord
Blessed be Your name

Blessed be the name of the Lord
Blessed be Your glorious name

Blessed be the name of the Lord
Blessed be Your name
Blessed be the name of the Lord
Blessed be Your glorious name

You give and take away
You give and take away
My heart will choose to say
Lord, blessed be Your name

10:11 p.m.

Though I was overwhelmed by Denise's piano performance there were additional noteworthy events today. She spent very little time reminding me of her desire to go home and how much she dislikes the hospital. Rather, she asked to play piano and to have me bring her chalk pastels so she could do some art. Her entire demeanour was far more positive though I must remind myself that can change from day to day. Still, it was nice to see her making the most of her situation instead of yearning for some other situation. That may change again tomorrow, but it was delightful to see her come alive today.

We got so see little Isabel twice today. That is a treat for Denise and almost certainly helped her outlook on life.

We obviously went out and about on the wheelchair. In fact, we went completely out of the hospital. The wind was too much, though, so we were back inside within a minute. Still, that is the first time she has been outside of the hospital since this all unfolded on April 16, eleven days ago.

She had a few guests (all family this time) but one of the highlights was playing "go fish" with her kids. It was a great way to both connect with her kids and slightly stretch her brain prior to the hard work of rehab.

On the medical front, the last tube in her body, the IV, was pulled and not replaced. The plan is to remove the heart monitor tomorrow and then she will be completely probe and tube-free! At that point it really is time to just focus on getting back up and running again for general life stuff. The OT and PT get the weekend off so there's nothing to report there. More news on Monday I am certain. I'm expecting her OT to be rather thrilled at her piano recital! Maybe she'll even have some art to show him.

New prayer item: her diet. She lost a bit of weight through all this and needs to gain it back with a balanced diet. I won't bore you with details; just pray that she eats the right amount of food and the right kind of food.

Continuing prayer items: mobility, neuro-recovery, patience, and as the poem says, the serenity to accept the things she cannot change.

By the way, Denise is now aware of the fact that she is something of a Facebook celebrity despite having no account on Facebook nor any desire to join. She will probably recite a message that I will type and post, maybe tomorrow.

April 28

10:13 a.m.

Today is starting out very sunny like yesterday. Denise is making plans for herself that involve her own personally guided and motivated recovery. She still gets a little bothered by her lack of energy and the fact that she's in the hospital but she is looking toward the future, taking initiative, remaining generally optimistic and putting in as much effort as her body can provide. Her eating continues to improve (but we're not there yet...).

When I arrived in the morning she had already decided that she was going to go for some walks today. She had already realized that she might not be able to make it as far as she would like so she already created a solution; use the wheelchair as needed. Thinking ahead, goal oriented, problem solving; she's doing pretty well, I would say!

April 29

7:36 a.m.

I arrived before Denise woke up so I thought I'd do a quick note. Should be an exciting day if she does end up moving to the brain injury unit and her doctor said she's ready to go. We just need to see if they have a spot for her. It's her last stop before getting out of here, but it is a long stop; several weeks. She has shown what I consider to be remarkable improvement in the past few days but we'll see what her PT and OT think.

She is now completely tube, needle and probe-free! Considering all the "accessories" she acquired when she arrived on the 16th this is progress indeed. She just has the ICD implant but she'll have that for the rest of her life which, I think we all agree, we hope will be a particularly long life.

Yesterday was great for her with lots of fun visitors. She played "go fish" with her kids again; always a highlight.

Prayer items include the usual; patience, a sunny disposition, perseverance for the hard OT and PT work that is ahead of her, and good rest when she needs it. A balanced and sufficiently large diet as well as strength (physical and mental).

10:32 a.m.

Denise does not have a Facebook account nor does she care to get one. As such, the following is a message she has dictated to me in order to pass it along to the Facebook world.

Paul suggested that I should write something to all of you guys. This is the first time that I've actually seen that Facebook could have a good purpose. Paul says there are hundreds of people keeping track of what's going on with me. That seems amazing. Thank you for all your prayers. I am getting better and feeling more positive about being able to do things on my own. I still need a lot of rest. I need patience to wait to go home. I don't like being told when I can't do things, like drive, especially for long times so I'll have to find creative ways of doing what I want.

Other than that I am most excited to get home.

April 30

10:04 a.m.

Quick update this morning. After eating a decent breakfast and getting cleaned up she went for a short walk and wheelchair ride to see the physiotherapy area in the hospital. Napping now.

Haven't seen doctors or OT/PT yet but we were told that whole process should get fired up fairly intensely today. Still curious when she's getting relocated to new unit. Will keep everybody posted.

Prayer requests:
- More energy to keep her going through rehab.
- She has a pain in her right side that may be a leftover from CPR.

Tylenol doesn't always help, prayer just might!

- She seems to be getting a progressively better outlook on life but please pray that this continues. She still has her moments of frustration.

Also, I'm going to start accepting people's offers for prepared meals in our freezer. The kids are at home at nights now and we're trying to do suppers together so that would help. Basic meals are best. Macaroni and Cheese dishes or some variation would be great. Chicken or beef dishes are great. Something we can stick in the oven and heat up would help a bunch. Contact me to organize. The kids and I aren't into exotic foods with unusual spices and what have you, just the basic stuff. I should be home most evenings if you want to drop them off then.

Speaking of the kids at home they had their first night in their own beds last night. I had to get them to school all by myself! It worked well, but it'll take time to get back into a really normal routine. They seem to be handling all of this marvellously.

12:15 p.m.

First OT/PT session in less than an hour. Pray for energy and focus. It will be the most intense thing she's done in weeks!

2:14 p.m.

First real OT/PT session is done. Very encouraging. More details later, but just know that it went well and she is showing major progress already and they haven't really started therapy until today!

8:23 p.m.

So I wanted to update a little about Denise's first real foray into Occupational Therapy and Physiotherapy. We actually went down to one of two rehab centres in the hospital instead of them coming up to Denise's room. Quite the setup! First the ever-lovable OT met with Denise. After doing a little probing of Denise's recent past (today and yesterday) he mused openly with his colleague that Denise might be ready for some very specific memory test that he doesn't usually administer until they are a little further along. I think it was called Rivermead for those who know what all that is about. He was clearly impressed with her memory improvement because he specifically said he usually waits a while before using that particular test.

Denise tried a little typing. Like her writing, it was packed full of strange typos but the OT was clear that the amount of correct typing she did relative to the errors was encouraging. She also tried playing the keyboard a bit but we decided she would try again with some sheet music.

All in all it was a good session that showed she has already made immense progress without having actually done any rehab yet! He gave us some insights into what to expect at the next unit (whenever she gets transferred!) which I think we both found helpful. She'll get to make herself lunch later this week and she was assigned some homework.

Then it was time for PT. Denise started with stairs. Easy. Stair stepping patterns. Easy. Stepping up two stairs at once, sideways. A little more difficult but still very manageable. Then we moved to the soccer ball. She had to demonstrate control and balance on one foot as she and I passed the ball between us. Relatively easy. All the tests showed that she had pretty good control, balance and sufficient strength. A little wobbly at times, but definitely fairly steady. She encouraged us to go for walks outside of the hospital. Of course, as I type this the snow is gently falling. Again. Seriously?!

The general message from both disciplines was the same; she is progressing very well. It was about an hour in total and she was fairly exhausted and glad to return to her room. Not surprising at all, and she did really well with everything. She'll get plenty more of that at the next unit so she'll need to continue building her energy over the next few days and weeks. She's getting sick of her mom telling her to eat protein, but this is one of those times a person really just needs to listen to their mom!

Otherwise the day was filled with a variety of fun visitors, some time gallivanting around the hospital in a wheelchair, an uneventful visit from the cardiologist on the unit, some time with her kids, and a nap. Typical for this stage of the healing.

No changes in the prayer requests from previous days. We're into the long and relatively predictable stretch so there shouldn't be any real surprises in the kind of help we'd like from Jesus at this point. I'll still keep everybody posted along the ride.

May 1

9:13 a.m.

She's moving units! Last stop, here we come... [38]

1:34 p.m.

A somewhat candid photo of the firemen who were responsible for saving Denise's life. This isn't the exact crew, but it's pretty close. One extra person who wasn't there that day and one person missing who was there. The paramedics didn't come for this visit.

May 2

7:10 a.m.

Today we start into her scheduled routine. She will have three or four therapy sessions each day and will need rest time in between. Until we get a sense of how her energy levels hold up in response to therapy (she is still

---

[38] To this day Denise remembers very little prior to May 1. She still describes this entire episode as something we went through, not her. Most of her knowledge of the heart-wrenching stuff she acquired by asking us about it, or reading the Facebook updates.

usually very tired after these things), if you are thinking of visiting please plan to come in the evening after the day's activities have wrapped up.

As usual feel free to get in touch with us at any time to plan ahead for a visit. If I don't follow up on the request please nag me about it. I'm juggling a lot of stuff right now and I am prone to forgetting some things. I'll need reminders on occasion.

I also got to thinking more about frozen dinners for the kids and I. I already mentioned pasta dishes along the lines of macaroni and cheese in a Pyrex dish or something. Pizza would be another great idea; pre-make it and then freeze the slices. Again, don't get too exotic with the toppings, we like pretty simple stuff. I'm not very imaginative with food (Denise usually takes care of that) so hopefully that gives you some ideas. Thanks, again, for helping in that regard. I'm home most evenings; just drop me a line before coming by.

5:06 p.m.

Today she really dove into therapy sessions. They are still working out her schedule and plan but it looks like she will have physiotherapy, occupational therapy, speech therapy (it involves much more than just speech; more in a minute) and recreational therapy. Yes there is actually therapy for recreation. I guess people need to relearn how to have fun!

For her first PT session she absolutely nailed it. Every balance test, every walking test, even doing stairs, she met every single challenge with ease.

Speech therapy also involves reading and writing; it's about comprehension, communication and reasoning in general. She performed virtually flawlessly in this area as well, though the initial test was a fairly basic test. I'm pretty sure there's some work to be done here too.

Recreational Therapy didn't meet with her today. I guess she'll learn paintball and MMA another time.

OT still needs work but she makes noticeable improvements every day in this area. In my estimation this will be the biggest area for regrowth in all her therapies. Even so, her improvement on her own is remarkable and she is never absolutely stumped and bewildered at any of the challenges she is given. She stumbles a bit, but the strategies and solutions to the challenges are in her mind somewhere. She just needs to relearn how to get her brain to play nice with her mind. It's coming!

Her days will be packed full. Visitors should expect to come after supper in the evening as a general rule (exceptions can occasionally be made) and you should expect to only stay for half an hour at most because she is receiving a lot of stimulation every day through therapy. She will normally be exhausted after all her work and visitors require a bit of energy as well. She enjoys the company, but it's time to pay closer attention to her energy levels and stimulation. As always, contact us to see about making it happen!

Prayer items:

- Diet. She needs more energy so she'll need to eat more in order to build up her energy. She doesn't always eat a lot; she needs to eat enough to meet her energy needs.
- Stamina. She's just tired a lot. Part of it is diet but part of it is lack of activity for the past several weeks.
- Focus and dedication. She seems to be fairly well focused and dedicated right now, pray that continues.
- Day passes. This unit encourages the occasional temporary discharges for people to get out of the hospital and get back into "real life," even if only for a few hours or a day at a time. I think she would benefit from this at the right time. Pray that we know when the right time comes and that all the necessary paperwork is in order to make it happen.

I will spend less time at the hospital in the near future as she gets into her routine and essentially "goes to work" every day. As a result, updates will probably arrive even less frequently than they have been. This is the longer-haul portion with a low likelihood of anything immediate and earth-shattering to report.

May 3

10:09 a.m.

I went for a date with my wife this morning. We had breakfast at the illustrious and highly recommended Chez Hospital Restaurant. You work with what you've got!

Even this small step was unimaginable only two weeks ago.

7:35 p.m.

It's the weekend and all the rehab staff go home so there will be no medical developments until Monday. With that in mind I thought I'd do a little recap of the big picture.

The doctors have addressed the heart issues to their satisfaction. Of course her heart will continue to be monitored for the rest of her life and various medications may come and go over the years, but with the ICD and her current meds they are happy with what they see at this time. She is completely unplugged from any tubes, probes or lines and has been for a while.

Rehab progresses and even today she told me that she did some tasks better than yesterday. The improvement is daily and easily observable. In fact she walked a distance today that's probably equivalent to a city block (and back) and she was outside where the ground is not perfectly flat. Math challenges today were tackled with greater ease than yesterday. In all areas of rehab the message is constant improvement, but still much to be improved upon in certain areas.

Next Wednesday we get a meeting with all the doctors, nurses and therapists associated with Denise's case. It's a one-on-team meeting where we just talk about Denise, her status and prognosis; no other patients will be present. It should be an interesting meeting because they ought to have enough data points by then to make a reasonably informed assessment of her condition and rate of improvement. We should get some pretty clear answers at that time, I hope. Of course nothing is ever certain in the world of medicine, I get that, but that meeting should give us our clearest view yet into the fog of medical speculation.

Prayer items aren't really changing a lot at this point so I'll keep them brief for ease of remembering:

- Energy for her therapies
- Sufficient food and rest
- Patience and perseverance
- Pain. Her chest still hurts sometimes from the CPR,[39] and her shoulder occasionally hurts from the ICD surgery.

Have a great weekend, all, and I'll let you know what next week looks like when we get there. May you all enjoy your respective loved ones as much as we have been enjoying our loved ones lately. Relish them. Seriously, think carefully about what life would be like without various members of your family and then treat them accordingly. We almost lived that out and I can assure you that you will look at your loved ones differently if you deeply ponder their mortality and consider their eventual demise. It's morbid, yes, but it quickly and effectively clarifies our priorities

---

[39] As an aside, not one of her ribs was broken. I was always told that if you are doing CPR correctly you will break some ribs. Her CPR was being done by professionals, yet none of her ribs broke. I found that interesting.

in life.

It can happen in an instant. You may not see it coming. Think about it. Act accordingly.

Make it count.

May 5

8:03 p.m.

So Denise had her first two days at home thanks to the unit's willingness to grant her "day passes." We picked her up Saturday morning, dropped her off Saturday evening, picked her up Sunday morning and just returned from dropping her off again. Next weekend we hope it will be a "weekend pass" which would include overnights and would be far more convenient.

The kids were pretty thrilled about having her at home, even if only temporarily. They also enjoyed coming along to bring her back to the hospital at night so they could spend as much time with her as possible. They absolutely cherished having her around.

Not too surprisingly, Denise spent a lot of time lying down and/or napping. We didn't go for any walks or bike rides or anything, but we did have some great family time eating outside and enjoying the warm weather. We kept guests to a minimum, for obvious reasons, but Denise enjoyed the very few who stopped by briefly.

But now the weekend is over, it's back to rehab, an intense week of therapy before we get to take her home for a little longer next weekend. Hopefully. Even next weekend, though, we expect her to spend a great deal of time catching up on sleep. Let's just hope (and pray) she has enough energy to focus on her rehab and that their therapy is as therapeutic as they intend it to be. In so many ways she shows far more improvement than I could have imagined possible. She remembered some events from only one week prior to her collapse. That seems pretty good to me considering she was previously a little sketchy about which century we were in!

May 6

5:10 p.m.

Just a quick update because I only saw her briefly today. I actually went to work for a few hours! I pedal-biked all the way and I treated myself to a blizzard on the way home, so for all those people who are concerned about me taking care of myself through all this; don't worry, I got it covered!

She is doing so well in PT that they seem to be suggesting that they don't have much more to contribute to her rehab. Of course PT is not the only therapy on the go, but it's encouraging to hear one of them already suggesting she's nearing the end.

She had a memory test that it sounds as though I would almost certainly fail. She did wonderfully.

She has been much more awake today. She skipped her nap due to a nurses meeting that was long and loud right outside her door, but she seems to feel fine nonetheless per her own words. She commented that today she has felt more awake than she has in a while.

She'll have a few more visitors tonight, hopefully a good rest (no more nurses meetings in the hall) and then it's back at it tomorrow. Also, they have made arrangements for the kids to help with her OT on Friday because they get out of school early. They are going to work together to make grilled cheese sandwiches for lunch! How much fun is that?

No, seriously, it's a legitimate medical therapy...

She is starting to get an odd pain in her other side, so pain is a continuing prayer item along with the others that have been previously mentioned (energy, patience, hard work, therapeutic success).

May 7

2:52 p.m.

Quick prayer request regarding pain. Denise is getting additional pain in her left arm. It went from a minor annoyance to being a pretty significant pain even after pain meds. It is actually slightly hindering her rehab so getting rid of it would be very helpful. Thanks.

May 8

12:37 p.m.

So this is a pretty major update on Denise's situation. Part of the protocol of the rehab unit she is on is to have a "family meeting" early in the rehab process. That took place this morning. The purpose of the meeting is to get the patient and their family around the table with the therapists, social worker, doctors and other specialists involved in her case. The medical staff went around the circle and shared their assessment of her present status, her progress, her prognosis going forward and they collectively provided an estimate of how long she'll need to stick around before being discharged. They also gave a bit of a snapshot of what the outpatient therapy will look like which was helpful as well.

The most common observation from everybody was Denise's low energy level. She regularly feels quite beat and her lack of energy is sometimes (not too often) limiting her ability to fully engage in the rehab. It's more often a case of her being able to complete the rehab and then she's just done right after it. Her stores are drained; nap time.

With respect to the brain rehab portion, however, they all agreed that she is back to a state of being functional and safe to go home. But for Denise that is setting the bar too low, which is part of the reason they want to keep her around. Given her progress thus far, and given her previous lifestyle as a teacher, mother and so forth, they want to push her far beyond the minimal level of "functional and safe." That is what they will focus on until she is discharged and that will be the focus of her outpatient rehab as well. In other words, their goal is 100% recovery, though time will tell if we hit 100% or something in the high nineties. She's currently trending nicely in that direction!

From a physiotherapy perspective (body motion, control, balance) there were no concerns. During the remainder of her time here they will push her, like the brain rehab portion, to attain something close to her previous lifestyle. They will try turning the walks into small hikes so the terrain will be less flat and the duration a little longer. This should also partially address her energy level issue, it is believed.

There is a concern that one of her meds may be impacting her energy level. She was on this med many years ago and it just drained her so she was switched to a different, but similar, med. The doctors will slowly, incrementally, adjust the meds but frankly this is not the kind of thing you want to get wrong. Wisdom is needed there, obviously!

Gerry asked if Denise's recovery is typical of what they see for people who go through what Denise has been through. The four therapists, almost in unison, shook their heads vigorously and said, "NO, this is quite unusual!" The general message of their subsequent comments was that Denise is clearly progressing much further and much faster than they would expect a patient in her situation to progress. That was very encouraging to all of us.

This weekend Denise will get an "overnight pass" which is not yet a full "weekend pass." Because of her low energy levels they don't want to give her a full weekend just yet, and warned her to pay careful attention to how much she puts into her weekend, but she will at least get to sleep at home from Saturday to Sunday morning. We won't be going to church (probably not for several weeks yet) and we'll have to be cautious with how much activity we plan for the weekend.

In terms of estimated discharge date, they figured it would still be probably in the range of two more weeks. They didn't pin a day at this point, but all indications are that it should be later in May instead of extending into June. As much as Denise isn't a fan of being in the hospital I think she is growing aware of the value that the rehab will have on restoring her to her former self. It's a long time, but she seems to be accepting that reality and working with it.

The pain in Denise's arm is not surprising given the implanting of the ICD. It will take some time to heal and pain meds will be available for as long as she needs them.

Prayer items (similar to before):

- Increased energy.
- Reduced pain in left arm.
- Wisdom as the doctors continue to tweak her meds.
- Patience for the next couple of weeks.
- Focus and dedication during her rehab.

We have much to thank God for already, and we will have much more to celebrate when she is discharged, but there is still a fair bit of road ahead of us before we are out of the woods. Jesus has been gracious through this journey and we are excited to see what he has in store during this final phase of this chapter in Denise's life.

4:44 p.m.

Funny story. Denise was playing Blokus with her recreational therapist and she won. Her RT was sincerely surprised and disappointed because she's never lost to any of her patients! I'm pretty sure she wasn't rigging the game either (especially if she normally wins). If that's not a sign that the brain damage is being repaired I don't know what is.

Here's to more victories, large and small!

May 10

7:33 a.m.

It occurred to me that I've been churning out prayer requests like they are going out of style but I haven't been specifically sharing answers to prayer. This will hardly be an exhaustive list, and some of these answers many of you will already be aware of, but here are some answered prayers that come to mind. Not all of these prayer requests were shared on Facebook, but they were answered anyway.

- She had her cardiac arrest in favourable circumstances. She was in the company of those who care for her deeply (strangers do not always initiate CPR) and we have several good reasons to believe that she was discovered very shortly after it happened. As long as we have known about her heart condition we have prayed for safety, this was God's way of answering that prayer; let her have her cardiac arrest under favourable circumstances.

- Her heart started again. It is hard to overstate the significance of this fact. Statistically it is quite rare for a heart to start again even with CPR, defibrillators and all the best medical care. The odds were very much against her.

- She woke up. Again it would not have been much of a medical surprise if she would have just remained comatose even after restarting her heart and breathing.

- She suffered minimal neurological damage. Some people come out of these things in FAR worse condition than Denise has.

- She has regained control of her body and is relearning skills (like piano).

- She has been rapidly healing and so far is blasting through therapy like there's no tomorrow. Her therapists agree that her progress is far from typical.

- Her early signs of mild depression have all but disappeared.[40] She no longer pines for home (though she's still excited to go home!) but seems eager to work her way through rehab.

- Her pain in her right side is subsiding. She recently got a new pain in her left arm, so prayer is still needed there.

We are told by Jesus that we would perform signs and wonders like Jesus himself did. As well as the "mundane" signs and wonders of feeding the hungry, clothing the naked and taking care of the helpless (you know, the usual culture transforming stuff) through Denise's story we have also seen a different kind of sign; something else to wonder at. Not only have we seen it, we have participated in it. If you have been lifting these prayer

---

[40] This statement was a little premature. She had a bit more of a journey ahead of her in this regard.

requests to Jesus then go find a mirror and tell yourself that God did something amazing through you.

Jesus said we would heal the sick. If you prayed for Denise then God used YOU to heal the sick.

Jesus said we would raise the dead. If you prayed for Denise then God used YOU to raise the dead.

These are not metaphors. I am not speaking figuratively of being raised spiritually or any other such thing. This is literal, physical. Denise's heart stopped moving blood. It is moving blood now. She was dead; now she is alive and well. If you prayed for her restoration to her former self then this was a joint effort between Jesus and you and the rest of those who prayed.

God raised and restored the dead through YOU! If that doesn't brighten your weekend I'm not sure what would.

May 11

6:25 a.m.

We pick Denise up this morning for the weekend. As usual we have very little planned for the weekend, but we're hoping the forecast is right; warm weather and sunshine. Because I don't update as often these days here are a few snapshots from the week.

I already mentioned that she beat her RT at the board game Blokus. I happened to take an elevator ride with her RT and we chatted about it. Yup, she beat her fair and square. Her RT plays somewhat regularly with her patients yet Denise has probably only played a couple of times in her life. Her RT has not recently suffered brain damage, Denise has. Given what should have been an obvious advantage in favour of the RT this turn of events was so surprising that her victory is now part of her medical record!

On Friday our kids had the opportunity to help Denise with her OT. They made lunch together; grilled cheese sandwiches. Getting the kids to help makes therapy all the more enjoyable. The kids got to play with some therapeutic hula hoops. This time they were used for non-therapy reasons.

Denise has been playing the piano a bit more as part of therapy. Her songbook is at the hospital. The other day she played the worship song, "A perfect heart" in the chapel. She got to play on the grand piano in McCaig tower.

She has been debating various subjects with her ST in order to confirm the higher functions in her brain and to help her word searching capabilities get back up and running. She still gets hung up on some of the less frequently used words in life, like "counterfeit." To help with that her ST gets into discussions with her on various subjects like the pros and cons of unions so she would have to access specific classes of words in order to have the discussion. Her actual opinions on the subject were obviously irrelevant, but her ability to engage the topic with only a few fumbles was very relevant.

PT is still great, though she had a little trouble doing lunges. I'm not sure how well she would have done with them beforehand either. It's not like she hits the gym, like, ever. She is part of a couple of "workout" groups now. The workouts are rehabilitating in nature (nobody is doing any bench presses or squats) so for her they serve the primary purpose of building her endurance. One such group works on hand strength and coordination which she joined this week.

Next week she can look forward to practicing C-Train rides (she cannot drive for six months after April 16), more debates and high-level thinking, piano and other endurance-building exercises. In other words, more of the same. On the weekend she'll mostly rest but she is planning on paying the bills as a bit of "homework" for therapy. This is something she always used to do in the past; she has taken complete care of our finances for years. That I haven't taken care of any of the bills while she has been in the hospital is not attributable to my laziness, nor the fact that this has been something of an overwhelming experience. It's because I'm a loving husband who anticipated how bill paying would be part of her therapy. No, really, I'm that thoughtful!

At this point in her recovery it's mostly about energy. Her body is still recovering; it did take a major beating after all. There is also still some regular pain around her left shoulder and her chest and every once in a while she gets minor aches and pains in new spots. Most of them just come and go and are a result of spending so much time in bed. Once her energy level improves so should a lot of those more annoying aches and pains because she'll get up and about a little more frequently.

As much as her general attitude about all this has improved (I still remember the first couple of days when she woke up – yikes!) she does still long to be at home and finds this entire thing frustrating.

Her memory is coming back well and I am starting to get the impression that some of the memories that she formed after her arrival at this unit about a week and a half ago are probably permanent. She vaguely recalls a few details from the previous unit but she is starting to clearly and unambiguously recall a lot more details from around the day she was transferred. That this is also the time her therapy took off in full force is probably no coincidence. She still forgets some things that happened on this unit – even visitors who hung out for a couple of hours at a time! – but she is remembering more than before and those memories seem to be sticking.

Most of the prayer items listed before remain, unchanged. As surprised as we were by very sudden and very positive results in the first week, this phase will be about long-term recovery and the results will take time and be far more gradual. We will need patience during the rehabilitation; patience for all of us.

Happy Mother's Day weekend everybody. I know this will be an unusually special Mother's Day for our family. As you hug your mom this weekend put yourself in the shoes of our kids and hug her with that kind of enthusiasm. On a personal note, our moms, Dorothy and Gerry, have been absolutely remarkable during this process. They have done more to help our family than we could have anticipated or would have dared asked for.

May 13

10:18 a.m.

Quick update. Denise observed that this is the third day in a row with minimal pain and minimal pain medications. She had her hand group therapy this morning which makes a point of using her weak (painful) hand and after it was done she was not in an unusual amount of pain. It hurt a bit, yes, but not unusually so.

It sounds like it is virtually guaranteed that she'll get a weekend pass this weekend. I think that means Friday night all the way to Monday morning. Considering Monday is a holiday perhaps Monday "morning" will be a particularly vague concept. We should get confirmation on Wednesday.

Same prayer items this week as past; mostly energy and pain. Pain seems to be subsiding, let's pray energy starts increasing.

Here's a funny story that still makes Denise laugh. When a patient needs some kind of non-medical attention there will be an announcement on the PA system that requests "Nurse or N-A to room..." N-A stands for Nursing Assistant. Of course the folks over the PA system do not always annunciate their words as well as they could, and the PA system isn't exactly the highest audio quality, so Denise spent days wondering why they kept calling for "Nurse Renee." Couldn't one of the other nurses help out? Renee seemed to get picked on a lot.

She still gets a chuckle out of that and she has no problem with me sharing it. When you talk with her, maybe just ask her how Renee is doing.

Weekend was great, will update more later.

4:35 p.m.

Thank you. You know who you are (I don't) and you know why. No questions, please.

8:33 p.m.

Some updates. The weekend? Great, but low energy. We actually had a lot more family stuff going on than we probably should have, but we just have such wonderful family. She did rest a lot, probably because of a lot more noise, activity and various forms of stimulation. As I already mentioned, on the weekend she started seeing a noticeable drop in pain which is delightful.

Back to the grindstone today. The group that works with hand strengthening and endurance went well. I peaked in at one point and I think I saw them working with nuts and bolts. She used both hands which made me very curious about how her ICD hand would respond. Would she be in greater pain? She was definitely a little more sore but, overall, it was still quite manageable.

PT – No surprises. A bit of a walk (no balance or coordination issues) and she was tired.

ST – Positive surprises! She had to do more debating and word searching and she did well. She was told, for instance, that she had one minute to list all the places she might buy a camera. She listed a good number of places; some I wouldn't have thought of. Other similar tests all with positive results and quantifiably superior results to the last time she did that kind of test.

As an interesting aside (and because this is a bit of a passion of mine) the ST seemed to have a clear understanding of what a debate is supposed to entail. She complimented Denise when she made a good argument, but didn't say anything when Denise just shared her opinion. Good on the ST for knowing the difference! Too many people today seem to think that a debate is all about exchanging opinions and preferences and hoping the other person will magically see things my way. It's about establishing a case based on evidence and reason; opinions should almost never play into it. And debates really don't have to be confrontational like many people think they inherently are.

If only somebody would write a book about how to argue with their friends, like, maybe ArguingWithFriends.ca. [Shameless self-promotion, I know.] I digress. Moving on.

OT – I missed this one due to poor planning on my part. I was told by her sister that she did very well. She was given a time limit within which she was to accomplish as many of the assigned tasks as she could. Nobody ever gets them all done in the time limit and that's not the point. This test was really a whole bunch of seemingly unrelated tests rolled into one and apparently Denise aced it!

No RT today.

The doctor poked her head in briefly and moved on without saying anything of significance. Obviously health issues related to her heart are not keeping her up at night!

The therapy plan this week is to get her out of the hospital a lot more. She will take at least two bus or C-Train rides to get some chocolate at a local mall and go for lunch with her family. She may go swimming as well another day. They recommended she come home some evenings so she'll have supper with us tomorrow night. Next weekend will involve a weekend pass and, because it's a long weekend, it will give us an unexpected additional day. Cool!

If all goes according to plan she's discharged next week. Wow, that was quick. Not according to her, of course, but according to pretty much everybody else involved in this process that's amazingly quick. I still remember Gerry saying it could likely take months for her to recover. I'm not saying my mother-in-law was wrong, I'm just saying... you know... that Denise is moving faster than... um... never mind.

Prayer items. Energy is still the primary problem on everybody's radar and the main reason she is still in the hospital instead of at home. Pain is subsiding but not quite gone. Another prayer item would be that during her times at home it would be very wonderful if we could detect any possible issues that rehab may not catch so that they can be properly addressed, even if it is through outpatient work. So far we have not seen anything they are not already aware of, but we need to keep a watchful eye on things. Pray we don't miss anything important.

May 15

10:18 a.m.

Today is a very sad day. I could not get the motorbike to start.[41] Very disappointing.

Oh, yeah, and Denise is fine. She actually came home for supper last night and got to spend some time with the kids doing homework and helping with piano and stuff. Not quite to her former standards but these are all steps in the right direction. We even briefly had a neighbor come and visit so that was a pleasant surprise for Denise and her friend.

She went to the mall yesterday via the bus. Just went, rested, and returned; no shopping. That was a full day. When she does get back home and people come to visit they are going to have to recognize her energy limitations. Today she has no special outings planned though tomorrow she is taking the C-Train to lunch (meeting her family) and on Friday she will go swimming. She should be good and wiped by the long weekend so it'll be fortuitous that she has extra time to rest and recover.

Therapist updates are the usual, "she's doing great." It's just energy. I'm starting to warn people that they might be somewhat shocked when they see her again. Other than needing more rest time than normal it will be pretty near impossible to notice any change from her former self. She still (rarely) gets stuck on random words here or there, but it's hardly noticeable in everyday conversation. It will almost be as if nothing happened. Sometimes her progress is so stunning that I have to mentally remind myself of what I saw about a month ago.

Speaking of one month ago, tomorrow will be exactly one month to the day since her cardiac arrest. And she's nearly ready for discharge.

Wow, that was fast. Jesus is powerful.

If only he would have let my motorbike start for me.

May 16

11:28 a.m.

Just a quick note that I am aware of the fact that a lot of things have fallen through the cracks in the past couple of weeks. If you contacted me to connect with Denise, or drop off food or something, or just to say hi but I never got back to you then that is not surprising. I'm not the most organized guy at the best of times and this has been far from the best of times so the ball is in your court. Harass me. Send repeated messages until I respond. I won't be offended or upset. That's what it's going to take right

---

[41] In hindsight this little attempt to introduce some lighthearted humour into the situation was probably poorly conceived.

now so just give 'er. Thanks for understanding.

5:18 p.m.

A couple of quick things. First, the motorbike started! I know that's probably been keeping a few of you up at night so I thought I'd get that out of the way. I know, we can all rest easy now.

Secondly, Denise continues to improve, but this time her improvement is not merely "Oh, she's doing well," but is of the variety that is inspiring three out of four of her therapists to conclude that she does not need any outpatient therapy! Of course she is not fully recovered yet, and she will not be fully recovered when she is discharged, but their conclusion has now become that outpatient therapy is unlikely to add any value to her recovery that normal life would not naturally add. That is exciting. The only therapist who is still waffling is her speech therapist.

Speaking of speech therapy (pun intended), I found her ST time today very interesting. She is quite obviously still have some issues with words, word finding, and even a bit of spelling. She was given a list of words with three spaces next to each of them within which she was to write synonyms for each word. No problem. The next list of words was harder and she was to write one synonym and one antonym. Here she fumbled a bit more. Her ST pushed a little bit on this and got her to focus on the more difficult words. Next was a list of definitions with spaces next to them to put the word associated with the definition; she was given the hint that all the words would end with "ine." For instance, "routine," "decline," and so on. A bit more difficulty here too. The last exercise is too difficult to easily articulate without seeing it, but it was really neat. Again, she stumbled a bit there too until she understood what was expected.

Included in all this were (if I remember correctly) only two spelling errors which is remarkably good considering where she came from, but again the typos were of such a nature to remind us that the linguistic part of her brain is still catching up. Continued prayer specifically on the recovery of her language skills is still in order.

Her energy level is slowly improving but it remains her greatest limitation. It is also very unpredictable. She was absolutely drained first thing in the morning but handled a three-hour outing fairly well after she had a nap. She was still relatively energetic when I left. It really comes and goes.

Pain has substantially improved. She has taken very few pain meds this week and nothing at all in the past two days. Her chest and shoulder still feel "off" but the pain is by no means debilitating.

She gets to go swimming tomorrow which should really push her stamina. I expect her to be drained by the time I take her home for the weekend. Fortunately we have kept our plans for this weekend to a minimum so she'll have lots of downtime.

May 17

4:33 p.m.

The plan is to discharge Denise on Wednesday. She may or may not have a little bit of outpatient therapy (not as much as originally planned) but most importantly she will be home with us, sleeping, eating and living in her house instead of at the hospital. As far as I am concerned, that will mark the end of this chapter of our lives. The drama began the day she arrived at the hospital, it ends the day she is discharged.

I do not intend to do any further Facebook updates about her progress after she is discharged because any further progress will mostly be incidental relative to the earth-shattering progress she has already experienced. If anything truly noteworthy comes up I'll mention it, of course, but I don't expect there to be anything really remarkable as she is already a stone's throw from fully recovered. I know my Facebook life has been "all Denise, all the time" but that will end.

Those of you who have kept up to date on her progress via Facebook have been part of this remarkable story, praying for her and encouraging her. I thank you for your involvement and I hope you are as delighted as I am to draw the curtain on this drama. Hopefully we can all get back to normal life again, though I hope we never forget the true value of "normalcy." Delight in the normal, don't let it become mundane!

I will always be available to answer any questions you may have about this epic tale, and I would be delighted to share Denise's inspirational story of hope and healing in your church or ministry. I hope to share this powerful story of God at work in human history. I believe Christians need to know what God is up to, and Denise's journey provides an astounding tale through which to draw attention to his sovereignty and the hope we have in him. In some small way I believe God wants to use this situation to bring him glory through what he has done.

I am also happy to go for coffee with people to explore the significance of these events and what it all means. I see the hand of God in all this, perhaps you disagree. Maybe you're on the fence about the whole thing. Whatever your thoughts, let's talk.

In terms of Facebook, though, I intend to dive back into the tedium of life before all this happened so there will be very little more about Denise. I will allow Denise to settle back into her normal state of relative online anonymity instead of being the centre of attention of my infinitesimal corner of the social media world.

Thank you all for your role in this tale of restoration. Your prayers and encouragement were instrumental. But now we can all breathe a little easier as we wrap up the denouement, offer our applause to the great story-creator behind the cosmos, and return to our duty of utilizing our daily lives to his glory.

We're almost there! Just a few more days. I'll keep updating right up to the moment she comes home. God bless.

May 18

3:43 p.m.

Minor update. Denise got a call that she is being moved to a different room for the final stretch of her stay. I don't know which room it is, but if you plan to visit her next week then either contact us before you come or ask at the nurses desk on the unit when you arrive. Don't just go to her old room.

Hopefully everybody is enjoying their long weekend!

May 19

5:44 p.m.

Another message from Denise. By the way, she will read comments so feel free to respond to your heart's content.

This will be my first ever post on Facebook. I am not a big fan, but have to admit that it has been an amazing resource during this time. I wanted to personally say thank you for all your support and prayer over this past month. Although I don't remember the first two and most intense weeks, I have heard the story from many different perspectives. It is clear to me that God was working in all this to make sure that this was a story to be told and not a tragedy.

Personally, I want to say thank you to those who came to visit in the evenings. I always found it hard to be on my own in the evening with nothing to do and those visits were wonderful. I know Paul kept good tabs on how many people came so I could rest so if you didn't get your chance to visit, thanks for your patience.

Updates:
- the pain from the surgery as well as the CPR is almost gone. This is a huge relief as I now feel like I can do things during my day without constantly dealing with and thinking about the pain.
- my energy level is slowing coming back. One day I went swimming with my rec therapist and another day I had a nap after simply having breakfast and a shower. I never know in advance when I'll be tired and when I'll have hours of energy. But overall, it's improving so I have to be thankful for the good stuff.

I am going home on Wed (permanently, as Cole says) and am already working on a new routine for myself. It will feel a little strange being home on my own every day, but I must remember that I'm still recovering, give myself time and truly enjoy the extra month of summer holidays!

Denise

May 20

9:49 p.m.

Weekend is over. Only two more sleeps and one more day (hopefully). Given how successful the weekend was I don't expect they'll want to keep her any longer. Her brain functions appear to be very well recovered on the whole and it's still just a matter of very low energy. She slept ten to thirteen hours each night and still needed naps!

May 21

4:33 p.m.

As the clock continues to wind down on this drama, some thanks need to be said. As much as I am certain that there is no way I will remember all the "thanks" that are in order for this whole episode I am equally certain that failing to even try is not a good choice. Considering all the ways that people have stepped up to the plate for our family in the past month some token of gratitude is needed.

First of all, thank you to all who prayed during this time. We were especially humbled when several folks in our church set up a 24-hour prayer vigil for Denise for a day. Other churches gathered around Denise's and her family; at one point it was raining pastors on our unit as so many people came to pray at her bedside. Jesus certainly chose to bring about the best possible results that medicine can provide and we know he always intends for prayer to be a part of that process. Do we have faith to ask? We did this time!

We must thank the staff at Denise's school, the paramedics, the firemen and the doctors and nurses in the ER for bringing her back to life.

We have to thank all the rest of the doctors, nurses and therapists for their work on her recovery. The improvement has exceeded all expectations, even of the veteran therapists.

Thanks to all who sent cards, flowers, gifts of various kinds as well as email and Facebook comments of encouragement and well-wishing.

Thanks to her many visitors. Although it is not possible for everybody to converge on the hospital it was wonderful to have people come alongside Denise as she recovered, and alongside us, her family, as we faced some terrifying uncertainty. Even simple things like times of coffee with friends meant a lot during this process as we digested all that was happening.

Many thanks (especially from me) to all those who brought food to the hospital or to my freezer. Denise was also delighted to have a steady stream of alternatives to hospital food.

Thanks to the staff at Denise's school also for the cards, flowers and various forms of video entertainment that have been sent along during her recovery. The majority of the gifts have been from Denise's students.

I know I have forgotten some people, but please know that even though my memory does not always serve me well, all of you did serve us well in big ways and in small ways.

10:08 p.m.

So here's the final real update with respect to therapists, etc.

PT – Did the six-minute walk test (a simple cardio test) a second time and substantially beat her numbers from last week. No outpatient therapy.

ST – Did a few more tests and decided no outpatient therapy is required.

OT – Met briefly and chatted about status and various going home issues. Gave Denise a nice, detailed list of homework but no outpatient therapy.

RT – Met briefly, confirmed everything looked good and decided she had to take one last shot at the reigning Blokus champion. RT won this time, but the margins were fairly slim, unlike Denise's crushing defeat over her last time! No outpatient therapy.

Doctor confirmed it's a matter of signing paperwork in the morning (he just returned from holidays). He will also compile a couple of pages of notes to summarize what happened on his unit (good to have). Should be out around lunch time.

It turns out that she will have some kind of outpatient therapy to go to; I think it's called cardio-rehab. She has not done that at all yet and I only vaguely understand what's involved so I won't try to explain it for fear of misrepresenting it. Still, I didn't get the sense this would be three times a week for the next eight months or anything onerous like that.

Everybody expects she'll be ready to go back to work in the fall but definitely not this year. Not enough energy (by a long shot) and she still has a bit of recovery of language issues. Nothing even remotely debilitating for everyday life, but she is a teacher so the standards are a bit higher, obviously. Now if she were an engineer, well, she could go back to work tomorrow. It is not as though we engineers have a propensity toward eloquence in the linguistic arts.

She will have various follow-up appointments on a variety of issues, but it's all of the "dusting out the corners" nature, or of the "looking far into the future" nature; nothing related to rehabilitation. Other than a bit of new outpatient rehab that I described, she's done.

After slightly over a month of tears, fears, hope, anguish, delight, perseverance and several other emotional twists and turns that I don't even have words for, the roller coaster is nearly ready to dock so that this band of seasick passengers can disembark. It's down to hours until this chapter of Denise's story comes to a close and the next chapter of her recovery begins.

As an aside, I just found out today through a friend that Denise's story was shared by a substitute teacher in a Catholic High School as s/he was teaching the class about the human heart. Denise works in an elementary school in the public system. How in the world...? My goodness, news spreads!

May 22

1:18 p.m.

On April 16 there were three little words I wasn't sure I would ever get to say. Today I am delighted to say them:

Denise is home!

The End.

The Beginning...

ABOUT THE AUTHOR

Paul is a husband and father of two. His formal training is in engineering though he has studied Christian apologetics and general philosophy for many years. He is also an inventor and an entrepreneur which has subjected him to even more, and entirely new forms of, suffering.

More information about Paul, and links to order his books, can be found at his personal website:

PaulKBuller.Wordpress.com

CPSIA information can be obtained
at www.ICGtesting.com
Printed in the USA
LVHW082010091222
734913LV00002B/169